Pilgrim Letters

Pilgrim Letters

Instruction in
The Basic Teaching of Christ

CURTIS W. FREEMAN

FORTRESS PRESS
MINNEAPOLIS

PILGRIM LETTERS
Instruction in the Basic Teaching of Christ

All Scripture quotations, unless otherwise indicated, are from New Revised Standard Version Bible, copyright © 1989 National Council of the Churches of Christ in the United States of America. Used by permission. All rights reserved worldwide.
Scripture quotations marked (NASB) are from the New American Standard Bible® (NASB), Copyright © 1960, 1962, 1963, 1968, 1971, 1972, 1973, 1975, 1977, 1995 by The Lockman Foundation. Used by permission. www.Lockman.org.
Scripture quotations marked (ESV) are from The ESV® Bible (The Holy Bible, English Standard Version®), copyright © 2001 by Crossway, a publishing ministry of Good News Publishers. Used by permission. All rights reserved.
Scripture quotations marked (GW) are from GOD'S WORD. GOD'S WORD is a copyrighted work of God's Word to the Nations. Quotations are used by permission. Copyright © 1995 by God's Word to the Nations. All rights reserved.
Scripture quotations marked (NKJV) are from the New King James Version®. Copyright © 1982 by Thomas Nelson. Used by permission. All rights reserved.

Cover Image: Christian Knocks at the Wicket Gate. The gate in the design is labeled by Blake: KNOCK AND IT SHALL BE OPENED. G. E. Bentley Jr., "The Inscriptions on Blake's Designs to *Pilgrim's Progress*," *Blake/An Illustrated Quarterly* 6, no. 3: 68–70. William Blake's twenty-eight watercolor illustrations for *The Pilgrim's Progress* were first reproduced in *The Pilgrim's Progress*, edited by Sir Geoffrey Keynes in 1941 by The Limited Editions Club, renewed in 1969 by the George Macy Companies, Inc., New York. The original watercolors are held in the Frick Collection, New York, New York. Public Domain.

Cover and interior design by Savanah N. Landerholm

Print ISBN: 978-1-5064-7050-4
eBook ISBN: 978-1-5064-7051-1

For

CURTIS RICHMOND FREEMAN

And Other Fellow Pilgrims on the Way

Therefore, since we are surrounded by so great a cloud of witnesses, let us also lay aside every weight and the sin that clings so closely, and let us run with perseverance the race that is set before us, looking to Jesus the pioneer and perfecter of our faith, who for the sake of the joy that was set before him endured the cross, disregarding its shame, and has taken his seat at the right hand of the throne of God.

Hebrews 12:1–2

Contents

Preface

THE WRITING OF THIS book came together very quickly, but it has been a long time in the making. I vividly remember the day our minister invited me for coffee to share his vision of writing a catechism for parents and children in our congregation. He reminded me that the Great Commission directs us to make disciples (Matt 28:19–20). "We are doing a pretty good job of baptizing them," he said, "but we are falling short in our obligation for teaching them to obey everything that the Lord commanded." It was a wonderful project that he completed and implemented and then encouraged other church leaders to take up.[1] At the time, I was aware of Catholics, Orthodox, and even some Protestants who provided catechetical instruction for new Christians, but I did not know many free churches that did. As I began to look more closely, I learned that catechesis was once widely observed across the denominational spectrum but over time had become a lost and forgotten practice. For the most part, it seemed that Sunday schools had gradually replaced the catechumenate. Although there are many reasons to commend Christian education in the church, it is not an adequate substitute for catechumenal instruction. As my minister friend alerted me

that day over coffee, "The church needs to recover the catechumenate." The ancient practice of catechetical teaching is
rooted in the apostolic tradition, which understands, as the
third-century Christian Tertullian contended, that we "are
made, not born, Christians."[2]

This book is grounded in the conviction that for the church
to be the church today, it must be committed to the practice
of making Christians. That may be a new insight, but it is
surely an old truth that must be reclaimed in every generation.
It demands a "new evangelization" that is not new in its basic
thrust but is new in the way that the gospel always renews the
church to adapt to changing times and circumstances.[3] For a
number of years, I have asked students in my classes to develop
a program of catechesis for those preparing to be baptized. I
have received great encouragement in reading their projects.
It is a sign of hope for a church that is committed to making Christian disciples, not simply receiving members who are
Christian in name only. One of those former students recently
gave me a cache of old catechisms that belonged to his minister grandfather. From the shape of their bent and worn pages,
it was clear that they had been well used in the ministry of
disciple-making. Sitting there in my office, perusing the stack
of booklets along with the pile of catechisms that I had already
gathered, I marveled at the simplicity of their doctrinal pre-
sentation. Yet their antiquated theological formulations and
archaic linguistic expressions rendered them ineffective tools
for passing on the faith today. I decided then and there to write
one myself. I designed this catechism to offer "instruction in
the basic teaching of Christ" for candidates preparing to be
baptized based on the six principles named in Hebrews 6:1–2:
repentance, faith, baptism, laying on of hands, resurrection,
and eternal judgment. This catechism frames the basic teaching in a question and answer format, one for each of the six

principles, which can easily be learned and discussed by cat-echists and catechumens, parents and young people, teachers and students.

A series of letters written by Interpreter, the catechist/teacher, to Pilgrim, the catechumen/baptismal candidate, follows the outline of the catechism. Any resemblance to C. S. Lewis's *The Screwtape Letters* is not entirely accidental. I regard those to be essential reading for thoughtful Christians, and the epistolary style immediately came to mind as a model for this project. Although his diabolical catechist is dedicated to leading souls to damnation rather than salvation, Lewis succeeds by engaging in satirical yet serious catechesis by way of negation. The theological and ecclesial scope of my *Pilgrim Letters* is evangelical and catholic, free church and ecumeni-cal, ancient and future. Yet in the interest of full disclosure, readers deserve to know that while I am deeply appreciative of the time-honored pedobaptist practice of disciple-making, which can be traced at least to the late second century,[4] I write as one who stands within the credobaptist tradition of bap-tism upon personal profession of faith, which, in the words of the Lima Document, represents "the most clearly attested pattern in the New Testament."[5] The letters provide a simple explanation of each principle, setting each practice within a broad biblical, historical, and theological context. Questions have been prepared for each chapter in hopes of leading to deeper reflection and conversation. One of the most striking features of the book is that each letter begins with an image from William Blake's illustrations of John Bunyan's *The Pil-grim's Progress* exemplifying the subject of the letter followed by an epigraph from the story that fits into the themes of the catechism. Bunyan's story has been a consistent source of inspiration and strength for me throughout my faith jour-ney, and Blake's images shockingly display the emotional, spiritual, and religious significance of Bunyan's narrative. I am excited to share these with new generations of Christian pilgrims.

I wish to express my thanks to friends and colleagues who read and commented on these chapters; to Elizabeth Newman, John Lockhart, Phillip Mumford, Sarah and Derek Hatch, Stanley Hauerwas, Fred Edie, George Mason, David Toole, and Kelly Sasser; especially to David Allen, who proofed the manuscript and contributed to the discussion questions and Jimmy Myers for preparing the indices. I offer a special word of thanks to Carey Newman at Fortress Press, who immediately recognized the importance of this project and saw it through to publication. I want to thank Debra Freeman, who during these strange days of Coronatide suggested that our family read these letters aloud and discuss the questions together. As I write these words during Holy Week, it is a challenge to remember that in baptism, we have been immersed in the suffering and death of the cross in the hope that we will be raised up with Christ into eternal life. As it so happens, our youngest son is himself in the midst of the catechetical process, considering the call to follow Christ into the waters of baptism. It is to him and others who walk this same path that I dedicate this book.

Curtis W. Freeman
Holy Week 2020

Catechism
The Six Principles

Therefore let us go on toward perfection, leaving behind
the basic teaching about Christ, and not laying again the
foundation: repentance from dead works and faith
toward God, instruction about baptisms, laying on of
hands, resurrection of the dead, and eternal judgment.

HEBREWS 6:1–2

Principle 1 Repentance

Q: What does it mean to repent?

A: It means that I have renounced the powers that would
control my life and am ready to start the Christian journey
that begins when I stop doing things my way and am ready
to follow the way of Jesus (Matt 3:2, 4:19; John 14:6).

Principle 2 Faith

Q: What is faith?

A: Faith is trusting that my life and all time are in God's
care and keeping because in the death and resurrection
of Jesus, the world has been made right (Heb 11:1–2;
John 3:16, 10:10; 2 Cor 5:7, 17–19; Rom 8:28–30).

Principle 3 Baptism

Q: Who should be baptized?

A: Having begun the Christian journey by turning my life over to God and trusting by faith in Christ, I am ready to be baptized in the name of the Father, Son, and Holy Spirit and to continue growing in the knowledge of what it means to be buried with Christ in a watery grave and raised to live in a new way of life (Matt 28:19–20; Rom 6:3–4).

Principle 4 Laying on of Hands

Q: Why does the church pray and lay hands on newly baptized Christians?

A: The church practices the laying on of hands with prayer upon baptized believers because baptism signifies the work of the Holy Spirit, which unites my life with Christ and with other members of his body and equips me with the gifts and graces needed to participate in God's mission to the world (1 Cor 12:13; Acts 8:17, 19:6).

Principle 5 Resurrection

Q: What is the hope of the resurrection for those who have been baptized in Christ?

A: Because I have been baptized, I am united with Christ in a death like his, and I hold to the hope that I will also share in a resurrection from the dead like his (Rom 6:5; 1 Cor 15:51–53). In life, in death, in life beyond death, I belong to my faithful Savior, and nothing can separate me from God's love (Rom 8:31–39; 1 Cor 15:54–56).

Principle 6 Eternal Judgment

Q: What is God's final judgment of those who are baptized and united with Christ?

A: I trust that in Jesus Christ, God has spoken both a life-giving yes and a death-dealing no to sin and evil, but I also trust that in his death on the cross, Jesus bore the no for all so that in his resurrection, all that remains is God's yes (2 Cor 1:19–20; John 3:17, 5:24). The Holy Spirit assures me that I am a child of God and an heir of God's promised salvation (Rom 8:16–17; 1 John 5:11–13).

Destitute
Ragged
Misery

Calm / Serene

Then Evangelist gave him a scroll with these words on it, *"Fly from the wrath to come."* When the man read it he said, *"Which way must I fly?"* Evangelist held out his hand to point to a gate in the wide field, and said, *"Do you see the Wicket Gate?"* The man said, *"No."* *"Do you see that light?"* He then said, *"I think I do."* *"Keep that light in your eye,"* said Evangelist, *"and go straight up to it; so shall you see the gate, at which, when you knock, it shall be told you what you are to do."*

Introduction

Basic Teaching

Dear Pilgrim:

For some time now, you have been thinking about being baptized. I appreciate the thoughtful way you have considered your decision. It is clear you have determined to be baptized not just because your friends did or because your parents might want you to. You want this to be your decision. I do too. Genuine faith must be free. It cannot be forced. That freedom is at the heart of what it means to be a follower of Christ. The second-century Christian Tertullian suggested that it might be best for people to hold off coming to Christ in baptism until they are capable of knowing where they are going and what they are doing: let them come, he urged, "when they have become able to know Christ."[2] It is still good advice even though we can never really know the full implications of what we are doing when we say yes to Jesus. Knowing Christ is not merely having a rational understanding of what it means to believe. It demands that we must learn what it means to be responsive to God's yes in Christ and to be responsible in the decision to be a Christ follower.[3] Baptism is a one-time event that only takes a few minutes to perform, but it requires a lifetime to learn what it means to be baptized. Please do not

1

misunderstand me. I want you to be a baptized Christian and a follower of Jesus, but my concern is for this to be a deliberate commitment on your part, not something that is forced on you.

This is the first in a series of letters I plan to write to you about what it means to be a baptized Christian. There are great mysteries of the faith that even the wisest theologians admit are unfathomable. Our consideration of those deep matters will have to wait for another time. My intent in these reflections is to provide you with an exposition of what the writer of the Book of Hebrews described as the basic teaching of Christ (Heb 6:1). This "basic teaching," which C. S. Lewis fittingly called "mere Christianity," is what I want to unpack for you.[4] You will find that you have already given some thought to these elemental matters. They are not new. These are things we have talked about and sought to practice in our homes for as long as you can remember. Hebrews names six foundational principles of the Christian faith: (1) repentance from dead works, (2) faith toward God, (3) instruction about baptisms, (4) laying on of hands, (5) resurrection of the dead, and (6) eternal judgment (Heb 6:2). It is certainly not an exhaustive list. Indeed, the fact that there are six principles is worth noting. Whenever the number *six* appears in the Bible, it signifies some incompleteness, which suggests that following the way of Christ does not stop with these truths. They are the end—the front end. They are the initiation, not the graduation. They lay a strong foundation to build on, but there is more teaching ahead. Yet this basic training in the faith is enough to get started or, as the writer of Hebrews put it, to "go on toward perfection" (Heb 6:1).

The early Christian church called this basic teaching *catechesis*, which means "teaching by word of mouth." One of the earliest examples of catechetical instruction after the New

Testament is in a book called the *Didache* (sometimes known as the teaching of the twelve apostles). It was a kind of manual for Christian converts. Prior to baptism, candidates were given instruction in the ways of life and death. The image of the two ways echoes the words of Jesus from the Sermon on the Mount, where he talked about the narrow road that leads to life and the wide road that leads to destruction (Matt 7:13–14). But it can be traced back to Moses, who described a way of life and a way of death. He urged the people of Israel to "choose life" by loving God, walking in God's way, and observing God's commandments so that they would live long in the land of promise (Deut 30:15–20). Jesus indicated his continuity with Israel when he said, "I am the way, the truth, and the life" (John 14:6 NKJV). And the earliest Christians called themselves followers of the way (Acts 9:2). What they meant was not just that Christianity is a way of life, though it certainly is. More importantly, they understood that to be a Christian is to be a follower of Jesus, who, in his person, embodied the way of life, which is the very source of life (John 1:4). The *Didache* summarizes that walking in the way of life means simply "to love the God who made you, and your neighbor as yourself."[5] To be baptized, then, means that you are prepared to follow the way of Jesus so that you might find the life that really is life (1 Tim 6:19). The eighteenth-century English preacher and poet Isaac Watts described the two ways in a hymn:

> Broad is the road that leads to death,
> And thousands walk together there;
> But wisdom shows a narrow path,
> With here and there a traveler.[6]

By the third century, the church had established an official period for the formation of those preparing for baptism, which came to be called the "catechumenate." During this time, which could last up to three years, the catechumens received instruction in the basic principles of the Christian faith. They also were encouraged to engage in basic Christian practices such as prayer, confession, fasting, caring for widows and the poor, learning the creeds, studying Scripture, and attending worship. The process culminated in baptism, often by full immersion, at dawn on Easter Sunday. As they emerged from the water, the newly baptized were given white robes, dramatically enacting the words of the apostle Paul, who wrote that "as many of you as were baptized into Christ have clothed yourselves with Christ" (Gal 3:27). These new members of the church were then invited for the first time to receive the Eucharist, or the Lord's Supper as it is typically called in the Free Church tradition.

Catechetical instruction was an important method for carrying out the reforms of the church in the sixteenth century. In 1529, Martin Luther produced his *Small Catechism*, which he encouraged pastors and teachers to use in the church.[7] Yet even more so, he urged families to use it for basic Christian instruction in the home. The catechism was Luther's attempt to state in a clear and concise way what the Scripture teaches. Its question and answer format provided an account of basic Christian doctrine that included brief summaries of the Ten Commandments, the Apostles' Creed, the Lord's Prayer, baptism, and the Lord's Supper, making it easy for parents to teach and for children to memorize. It became a model that other Protestants followed. Over the years, I have gathered a collection of catechisms that often were printed as small pamphlets. One of my favorites is *St. Paul's Catechism*, written in 1693 by Thomas Grantham, an English Baptist minister.[8] It is a conversation between a father and son about the same six principles from Hebrews 6:1–2 that I want to think about with you. Though the language is much more formal, it sounds very much like some of our talks. It is a good reminder that learning "the basic teaching of Christ" is not something to be done in church on Sunday only. Instead, it is a practice meant to be part of conversations in the home every day of the week.

This model of catechism as family conversation also shows us that the Christian faith is not something we make up as we go. It is an embodied wisdom that must be handed on from generation to generation. One Sunday morning in worship, I remember passing you the attendance roster. There were spaces labeled "name," "member," "visitor," and a few other items. You said to me, "I am not a visitor, but I am not a member either." "Yes," I said, "you are a catechumen." "What's that?" you asked. That conversation is in part why I decided to write a catechism and these letters explaining it. Most Protestants have given up the practice of *catechesis*. They determined instead that young people would learn the Christian faith primarily in Sunday school rather than at home. I am grateful that you have come under the influence of some excellent Sunday school teachers who are committed to the vocation of being Christian catechists, even if they may not have used that term to describe themselves. They were catechists because they were not so much concerned about providing age-appropriate religious education as they were committed to helping you understand what it means to be a Christian.

I also give thanks that I have friends and colleagues who have helped me understand the significance of recovering this lost practice of catechesis. When I was a participant in an ecumenical dialogue with the Catholic Church, I learned about the Rite of Christian Initiation of Adults (RCIA), which retrieves for Catholics (and Protestants too) the ancient practice of the catechumenate dating back to the third-century Christian leader named Hippolytus and his writings on *The Apostolic Tradition*.[9] I have continued to draw from that wonderful resource. Our former minister wrote a catechism for our congregation. That document was an excellent tool that created serious conversations among church members about what it means to pass the faith on to others. One of my former students who is now a pastor has led his congregation to put together a beautiful catechetical document they call *Via Karis*, which means the "way of grace."[10] It guides them in the basic teachings of Christ through practices of water, word, table, body, and creation. Learning to live the way of grace becomes a means to deepen friendship with God and one another through worship, education, mission, and fellowship. Being part of the catechetical practice like these communities helps us learn to live as Christians and know that we do not so much start a journey at the beginning as we join in with a community that has been on pilgrimage together over a long time. Saint Augustine described the church as a pilgrim community that lives as exiles in the present age but journeys by faith to their true home.[11] He traced that pilgrim community back to Abraham, who looked toward the city whose builder and maker is God (Heb 11:10). It is a reminder that we are not alone, because we travel with fellow pilgrims on the same journey.

The basic teaching of Christ laid out in Hebrews 6:1–2 is set within the scope of the whole book, which invites us to imagine ourselves as being on a journey like the people of Israel. As you know, after they left Egypt, they wandered for forty years in the wilderness before they reached the Promised Land. Surviving in the desert was not easy. Just finding food and water tested them to the limit. But Moses led, and God provided. They finally reached the end of their journey and entered their promised rest (Heb 4:1–11). Challenges await us too, and we need to be ready. Like the people of Israel, we will be tempted to stop or give up. But when discouragement finds us and when we struggle along the way, we find encouragement to keep going. Like Moses led Israel, Jesus leads the church. He has blazed the trail ahead. He is "the pioneer and perfecter of our faith" (Heb 12:2). And he understands our every weakness because he was tested to the limit just as we are. Yet Jesus remained faithful to the end (Heb 4:15). Let us then follow Jesus with the confidence that God will provide, giving us strength to continue until we reach our journey's end and enter our promised rest. As you think about following Jesus on this pilgrimage, the six principles of Hebrew 6:1–2 are the basic equipment you will need to be outfitted for the journey.

When I was about your age, I first read *The Pilgrim's Progress* by John Bunyan. I had no idea at the time that it is one of the most widely read books in the world. Some people have said that it is a classic text because it became a kind of prose epic for evangelical Christianity. There is some truth to that claim, but I think its wide appeal is more due to its popularity as a catechetical narrative. Bunyan presents the basic teaching of Christ in a story form that captures the imagination so that we see ourselves in it. It was so effective that wherever Christian missionaries went, after translating the Bible into the language of the people, the next book they often translated was *The Pilgrim's Progress*. It portrays the Christian life as a journey, filled with struggle and conflict but also full of faith and hope. Bunyan wrote a hymn that is sometimes sung in church. My favorite part is the last verse, which often gets changed or left out. I think it describes what it means to be a Christian.

> Hobgoblin, nor foul Fiend,
> Can daunt his Spirit:
> He knows, he at the end,
> Shall Life Inherit.
> Then Fancies fly away,

He'll fear not what men say,
He'll labour Night and Day,
To be a Pilgrim.[12]

My discussion of each of the six principles begins with a scene from *The Pilgrim's Progress*. I hope that in our conversations, you might begin to imagine your life in the story. The image that I selected for this letter is a conversation between Christian and Evangelist. Christian has just set off on his journey. Not knowing which way to go and weighed down with his heavy burden, he asks for directions. Evangelist points him to the wicket gate, which is a small door leading into the church. He tells Christian to knock on the door, where he will be given further instruction.

You have sought out toward that same place: "Knock, and the door will be opened for you" (Matt 7:7). As you make your way, rest assured that you are not alone. There are other pilgrims on the same road who will be excellent conversation partners. You will learn from them. But be careful because there are also people who will advise you that there is an easier way. Some may even try to get you to stop or turn back. Do not listen to them. They may sound persuasive, but there are no shortcuts to your destination. And their advice leads to trouble. Your best guidance lies on the other side of the door. And some of the most interesting pilgrims you will meet there are in the Bible. It is full of stories about people who traveled this way too. One story I would commend to you is about Philip, a Christian from Jerusalem, and a pilgrim returning to his home in Ethiopia (Acts 8:26–40). After a chance meeting in the desert, the two of them traveled together on a road from Jerusalem to Gaza. After a long and lively conversation on the basic teaching of Christ, the Ethiopian man said to Philip, "Look, here is water! What is to prevent me from being baptized?" (Acts 8:36). My hope and prayer is that your journey and conversations might lead you to a clearer understanding of the basic teaching of Christ and that at some point along the way, you might also ask, What is to prevent me from being baptized?

Yours in the journey,

Interpreter

I saw a man whose clothes were in rags, and he stood with his face from his own house, with a book in his hand, and a great burden on his back. I saw him read from the pages, and as he read, he wept and shook with fear—then he let out a loud cry, and said, "What shall I do to save my soul?"

Principle 1

Repentance

Dear Pilgrim:

In my last letter, I said that your best guidance about following the way of Christ lies on the other side of the door that leads into the church. When you cross the threshold of any Christian house of worship, you will discover that they are all committed to prayer, no matter how different their understandings and expressions of the faith. Yet it is not clear that they are of one mind about how to pray. For some, prayers are very formal and read in unison. For others, they are more casual and ad-libbed by individual participants. These differences, however, are more matters of style. The significant variations concern what prayer is for. It may seem that for some people, prayer is mostly about asking God for things. Do you remember in *The Adventures of Huckleberry Finn* when Miss Watson told Huck to go into the closet and pray every day and that whatever he asked for he would get? So he asked for some fishing hooks, but when he did not get any, he gave up on prayer.[2] When Jesus's disciples asked him to teach them to pray (Luke 11:1), he gave them a model prayer (Matt 6:9–13). The Lord's Prayer voices deep desires that should shape our lives and the way we see the world—for God's name to be hallowed in our living, for God's reign to come and God's will to be done on earth, for provision of daily bread, and for receiving and offering forgiveness. The *Didache* recommends praying it three times a day, which is not a bad idea.[3] I wonder what might happen if each time we washed our hands throughout the day, we were to pray the Lord's Prayer instead of singing the ABC song.[4]

In the last petition of the Lord's Prayer, Jesus urged his followers to pray for deliverance from evil (Matt 6:13). To pray for God's deliverance is central to what it means to practice repentance (Heb 6:1), which is the first of the basic teachings of Christ. When Jesus began his ministry, he called people to repent and believe in the good news that the reign of God was on the way (Mark 1:14–15; Matt 4:17). The apostles taught those who wanted to become followers of Jesus that they must show signs of repentance before being baptized (Acts 2:38). It makes sense, then, that repentance is the first principle listed in the basic teaching of Christ (Heb 6:1). The word *repentance* is not often heard outside of church. When it does occur, it is usually a caricature, bringing up a mental image of a scary-looking figure warning that if you do not feel really bad about all the awful things you have done, you will be in big trouble with God. That is not how the word *repent* is used in the Bible. It actually means something like "change your mind," although it is not simply a suggestion that all you need to do to get things right is to shift around a few opinions. It imagines a radically altered way of seeing life so that you no longer place yourself at the center of things. It requires a turning or reorientation so that the focus of your attention is in God's direction. In this sense, repentance is a deliberate openness to the sort of change Jesus described when he said, "If any want to become my followers, let them deny themselves and take up their cross daily and follow me" (Luke 9:23).

Repentance, then, is not simply a matter of feeling sorry about mistakes or even admitting them. It is a deliberate decision to forsake the path we are currently on and declare our commitment to follow Jesus wherever he might lead. This broader sense of repentance drove Martin Luther to declare, "When our Lord and Master Jesus Christ said, 'Repent,' he willed the entire life of believers to be one of repentance."[5] Repentance, like baptism, is not a one-time event. It is more of a process or a journey that takes a lifetime to work out. But it is also a deliberate and personal act. There is an old spiritual song that says,

> Not my brother or my sister, but it's me, O Lord,
> Standin' in the need of prayer.
>
> Not my mother or my father, but it's me, O Lord,
> Standin' in the need of prayer.[6]

Repentance is not something anyone can do for you. It has to be your decision. When a group of Christians met in Schleitheim, Switzerland, in February 1527, they formulated a document stating their basic beliefs. In the first article, they declared, "Baptism shall be given to all those who have been taught repentance and the amendment of life and who believe truly that their sins are taken away by Christ."[7] Baptistic Christians have followed this same practice. Edward Barber was probably the first English Protestant to embrace believer baptism by immersion, which he called "dipping." He stated that "they only are to be dipped that are made disciples by teaching."[8] On this question of the proper candidate for baptism, baptistic Christians of various sorts echo the cautious advice of Tertullian that people should be baptized "when they have become able to know Christ."[9] Some Christians have wondered if this implies that there is an "age of accountability" when a person reaches a point that they are morally responsible for their own actions. If there is such a thing, it cannot be identified with any particular chronological age because moral development varies from person to person. My friend and theological mentor Jim McClendon once said that a person is ready to be baptized when they can say no to their parents and peers. The fact that you have shown you can resist parental and peer pressure suggests you grasp why this is a commitment that only you can make. Putting repentance first stresses that a deliberate and personal commitment to follow Jesus before being baptized is crucial for ensuring that the church is above all a community of disciples.

Yet placing such a strong emphasis on personal commitment seems to assume that a decision to follow Christ is a simple matter. As you have already learned, it is not that easy. We make all sorts of commitments that we have every intention of keeping, but at the end of the day, we look back and realize we did not follow through. It is not just about small things either. We also have trouble keeping the big promises we make. It is not that we want to be irresponsible. There is just something about the human condition that makes constancy problematic. The apostle Paul described this inner conflict of wanting to do what is good but lacking the power to do it (Rom 7:21). One contemporary writer described this condition as the human propensity to mess things up.[10] It is not that we mess things up by accident. There is something about us as human beings that inclines us to break things—promises, relationships, even our own well-being. It is like Nurse Nancy in William Faulkner's *Requiem for a Nun*, who tries to explain why people do bad things even when they know right from wrong. "You ain't got to," she says, but "you can't help it."[11] We are caught in a web of debilitating and destructive habits that determine our lives in ways that are out of our control. The church has a word for this condition. It is called *sin*. The apostle Paul wondered how we might ever be free of this inner conflict. He concluded that we are not hopeless: "Thanks be to God through Jesus Christ our Lord!" (Rom 7:24–25). The church has a word for this divine help too. We call it *grace*. It is the good news that in Christ, God is for us. To put it simply, we are obliged to repent, but we lack the capacity to carry out our intentions. The good news is that God offers us the power to keep the promise we make to follow Jesus. When we realize our inability to do what we desire, God offers help. The answer, then, though it may seem oddly off, can be put in a simple sentence: "Let go and let God."[12] (Summer Camp 2022)

The struggle to follow Jesus is an inner conflict, but the forces with which we wrestle are not only within us. Our lives are subject to external powers beyond our control, and we must learn to resist them in order to make our journeys. The apostle Paul described this reality in apocalyptic language when he said that "our struggle is not against enemies of blood and flesh, but against the rulers, against the authorities, against the cosmic powers of this present darkness, against the spiritual forces of evil in the heavenly places" (Eph 6:12). I know it is not fashionable these days to talk about the devil and evil. But I think C. S. Lewis was right when he suggested that it is just as much a problem to disbelieve in the reality of evil as it is to have a fascination with it. Neither the materialist nor the magician is of much help in learning how to be free.[13] The powers are real, and we ignore them at our own peril. They are energies that are both visible and invisible, earthly and heavenly, spiritual and physical, personal and suprapersonal. They are expressed in and through social, political, and economic realities, but they are bigger than these forces or institutions or people or ideas.[14]

Our congregation has a covenant partnership with Iglesia Emmanuel in San Salvador. The members of Emmanuel Church know all too well the reality of these powers. Many of them remember the violent civil war that lasted from 1979 to 1992. It is estimated that death squads executed over seventy-five thousand people, including Catholic archbishop Oscar Romero, who was assassinated on March 24, 1980, while he was leading worship.[15] Romero has now been officially recognized as a saint because of his courageous witness against violence, corruption, and oppression. The war is over, but the violence continues as gangs regularly kill anyone who opposes them. It has been a powerful testimony for our congregation to learn from Christians who face violence daily but who seek to resist the powers by demonstrating how to live peaceably by modeling what it means to be forgiven and to forgive, as the Lord's Prayer teaches us. Yet the seductive work of the powers is often much more subtle. The people who crucified our Lord did not appear to be bad people. In fact, they all claimed to be standing up for something that seemed right. The scribes came in the name of the law, the Pharisees in the name of piety, the Sadducees in the name of the temple, Herod in the name of political stability, and Pontius Pilate in the name of social order. Had they understood their actions, none of them would have dared crucify him (1 Cor 2:8). Yet they all were complicit in his death, and they all were activated by forces beyond their own agency. But there is good news: God has "disarmed the rulers and authorities and made a public example of them, triumphing over them in [Christ]" (Col 2:15). That means Christ freed us from the powers that would otherwise control us. And through prayer, we learn to live into this freedom.

While the modern mindset may have trouble recognizing evil, for early Christians who found themselves subjected to oppression by "the powers that be," it was not merely a theoretical question. The practice of the ancient Church of Rome, in the literal belly of the beast, was for catechumens just prior to baptism to say publicly, "I renounce you, Satan, and all your service and all your works." The priest would then anoint the catechumen with "the oil of exorcism" and declare, "Let all evil spirits depart from you." Then the catechumen would pray for the grace to do God's will.[16] That strikes me as a practice worth recovering, because if we need to learn anything, it is how to be free from the powers that would control our lives. Whatever repentance is about, it is about being prepared to grapple with the forces that seek to divert us from our journeys. Christians must resist the forces that stand opposed to God's reign, but to mount a campaign of resistance, we must arm ourselves with the weapons of the spirit, which the apostle Paul calls "the whole armor of God" (Eph 6:11). We must take up the belt of truth, the breastplate of righteousness, the shoes of peace, the shield of faith, the helmet of salvation, and the sword of the spirit, which is the word of God (Eph 6:14–17). So we pray the Lord's Prayer, not out of a hopeless resignation to forces of fate, but to ask God the Father with Christ the Son for deliverance from the powers of control (Matt 6:13).

Another one of my favorite books is *The Life and Adventures of Robinson Crusoe*. It is about a young man who foolishly left home, not in a quest to find salvation, but in search of fame and fortune. He had not gotten far before he realized he had made a mistake. He wanted to turn back, but he simply could not admit he was wrong. Human beings, Crusoe observed, are such strange creatures who are "not ashamed to sin, and yet are ashamed to repent; not ashamed of the action for which they ought justly to be esteemed fools, but are ashamed of the returning, which only can make them be esteemed wise."[17] I hope you will not be ashamed to admit mistakes. Even more, I hope you will gain the wisdom that comes from repentance not just at the beginning of the journey but, as Luther said, throughout your whole life. As you seek that wisdom, I commend these words from Psalm 51. Let them guide your prayers of penitence:

Have mercy on me, O God,
 according to your steadfast love;
according to your abundant mercy
 blot out my transgressions.
Wash me thoroughly from my iniquity,
 and cleanse me from my sin!

According to the basic teaching of Christ, repentance, in the words of our catechism, "means that I have renounced the powers that would control my life and am ready to start the Christian journey that begins when I stop doing things my way and am ready to follow the way of Jesus."[18] Renouncing the powers is one thing. Being free from their influence is another. We are sinners, weak and vulnerable, powerless to free ourselves. Weighted down by our mortality and distracted by our tendency to wander, we discover along the way that this journey is more difficult than it appeared when we first began.

Repentance is one of the basic teachings of Christ because it is a lifelong practice. Every year, as we return to the Lenten season, Christian pilgrims gather for prayer on Ash Wednesday. The simple imposition of ashes reminds us that we are sons and daughters of earth. Though destined for another city, we walk here through the wilderness east of Eden with fellow travelers, seeking our promised rest (Heb 4:9–10). The desert fathers and mothers of the third and fourth centuries learned that they could only sustain the wilderness journey by continuous prayer (1 Thess 5:17). The substance of their devotion was these simple words: "Lord Jesus Christ, have mercy on me!" It confesses human weakness and invokes divine grace. The most dedicated of these spiritual athletes were committed to saying the Jesus prayer thousands of times each day. Many years ago, I read the journal of a nineteenth-century Russian Christian who told how he gained strength and endurance for his faith journey by praying this ancient prayer.[19] Praying the Jesus prayer, even for short periods, has strengthened my walk. But when callings and commitments hinder my prayer, I remember that I am part of the communion of saints that prays without ceasing. The story is told about an old monk named Lucius who each evening put two coins outside his door, saying, "Whoever finds these two pieces of money prays for me when I am eating and when I am sleeping," adding, "by the grace of God, I fulfill the precept to pray without ceasing."[20] Prayer is spiritual exercise that prepares us to endure the long journey. Yet when we cannot pray, we know that we are part of a worldwide community of prayer, the pilgrim people of God, which, along with the church at rest, prays with us and for us as we seek sustenance and strength to continue on the way.

The image from Bunyan's *The Pilgrim's Progress* that appears at the beginning of this letter is from the opening scene. It pictures a man, later called Christian, reading from the Bible. Weighed down with a heavy burden and under deep conviction, he asks with a profound sense of urgency, "What shall I do to save my soul?"[21] The answer in a word is "Repent." He must depart the city of destruction and embark on a journey to the Celestial City. This he does, leaving behind everything and everyone of comfort and security to set off on his pilgrimage. Repentance is the beginning of a long obedience that takes a lifetime to complete, and resistance to the powers that you renounce will require more armor. Just as Christian was outfitted later in his journey, so must we. And as Christian prepared to face Apollyon, wondering whether he should retreat or stand his ground, he remembered that there is no armor for the back, so turning around was not an option.[22] You have begun the journey. Keep your eye on the prize, the hope set before you, the city not made with human hands, whose builder and maker is God (Heb 11:10).

Yours in the journey,
Interpreter

Just as Christian came up to the cross, his burden loosed from off his shoulders, and fell from off his back, and began to tumble, and continued to do, till it came to the mouth of the grave, where it fell in, and I saw it no more.[1]

Principle 2

> *Faith*
> *in*
> *God*

→ *desiring to know the God we believe in*

↓

learning we can trust God

Dear Pilgrim:

The second principle of basic Christian teaching is "faith in God." Given that even in a secular age, the overwhelming majority of people still say they believe in God, it would seem safe to assume that someone preparing for baptism also believes in God.[2] But such an assumption confuses having faith in God with simply believing in God's existence. Faith is not just admitting we believe in God. It is desiring to know the God we believe in (Heb 11:6). None of us when we were infants wondered whether the strangers who we would later call our parents existed, but we were concerned about whether these strange people could be trusted. Over time, we learned to rely on their care. We did not ask them to prove their love. We took it on faith. Faith in God is something like that. We are confronted with the reality of a strange and mysterious Being whose beauty, power, and love are beyond anything we have ever encountered or could even imagine. We learn to identify and name this presence as God. Yet faith is more than believing that such a Being is real. Faith is learning that we can trust God, whose reality is the very source of our lives.

↓

The stedfast love of the LORD is from everlasting to everlasting

21

"Faith," as Hebrews puts it, "is the assurance of things hoped for, the conviction of things not seen" (Heb 11:1). Farmer-preacher and Bible translator Clarence Jordan fittingly described faith as "the activation of our aspirations."[3] Believing in an unseen reality might seem like just another way of saying, as the White Queen told Alice, that if you take a deep breath and shut your eyes, with some practice you can believe "six impossible things before breakfast."[4] That would be a mistake because it supposes that faith is just a mode of thinking. Faith is neither an absolute certainty based on the facts nor a blind leap into the dark. Faith is more a way of seeing, compelled not by the confidence that we understand but by the conviction that we desire what lies ahead. Faith is being drawn by the promise of a future toward which we move. Faith is a journey of seeking to know God—not to know about God, but to know God. What makes the journey exciting, and sometimes dangerous, is that there is no map. Yet there is a voice that calls out to us, like Abraham, telling us to leave the familiar place and seek a city whose builder and maker is God (Heb 11:8–10).

Anselm of Canterbury described this process of knowing God as "faith seeking understanding." The opening chapter of his book *Proslogion* closes with this prayer:

> Teach me to seek you,
>> And as I seek you, show yourself to me,
> For I cannot seek you unless you show me how,
>> And I will never find you unless you show yourself
>>> to me.
> Let me seek you by desiring you,
>> And desire you by seeking you;
> Let me find you by loving you,
>> And love you in finding you.
> I do not seek to understand so that I may believe,
>> But I believe so that I may understand;

And what is more,
>   I believe that unless I do believe I shall not
>   understand.[5]

Praying for God to increase our faith means that faith is not a one-time experience that settles everything for life. Instead, it is the beginning of an unfolding journey toward a fuller understanding. What defines us as Christians, then, is not so much what we think as what we believe, and what we believe is based on how we hope, and how we hope is shaped by what we desire, and what we desire is formed by the way we pray.

The good news is that we do not have to make things up as we go. Soon after the apostles died, Christians started putting together summaries of the faith. These ancient confessions of faith became known as "creeds" because of their defining words, "I believe" (*credo* in Latin).[6] They became a basis for catechetical training and have served as ecumenical statements of faith for the whole (or catholic) church. The one most associated with baptism is the Apostles' Creed, which declares,

> I believe in God, the Father almighty,
>   creator of heaven and earth.

> I believe in Jesus Christ, God's only Son, our Lord,
>   who was conceived by the Holy Spirit,
>   born of the Virgin Mary,
>   suffered under Pontius Pilate,
>   was crucified, died, and was buried;
>   he descended to the dead.
>   On the third day he rose again;
>   he ascended into heaven,
>   he is seated at the right hand of the Father,
>   and he will come again to judge the living and the
>   dead.

I believe in the Holy Spirit,
    the holy catholic Church,
    the communion of saints,
    the forgiveness of sins,
    the resurrection of the body,
    and the life everlasting. Amen.[7]

The first article of the creed begins with the declaration, "I believe in God." This affirmation does not end with a period. It continues by identifying the God we trust as the God of Israel, who is made known to us in Jesus of Nazareth, his Abba/Father, and their Spirit. In the name of this "three-personed God," the church joins the mission of making disciples by baptizing and teaching them (Matt 28:19), and in the name of this triune God, the church gives and receives benediction (2 Cor 13:13). The God that we believe in is not some mysterious abstract deity. The One in whom we place our trust is the three-in-one God named in the creed. This Trinitarian center grounds our faith and practice. It gives us the language to say with simplicity and clarity that when we say "God," we mean the Trinity—Father, Son, and Holy Spirit.[8] Confessing the ancient ecumenical creeds keeps our faith connected with the most basic and fundamental grammar of the faith in the triune God of historic Christianity.

Faith seeking understanding does not mean we understand. Faith is not the same as certainty. As one person said to Jesus, "I believe; help my unbelief!" (Mark 9:24). Faith is a commitment to seek understanding, more like "I do" than "I know." When, for example, we recite the words of the creed that we believe in Jesus Christ, God's Son, "born of the Virgin Mary," we are not claiming to understand what that means. We are trusting that by saying these words, we will grow in our understanding of what that means. These words are not meant to be an explanation of how God was in Christ. Instead, they give us the language to affirm that from the very beginning, God was in Christ, reconciling the world (2 Cor 5:19). Faith in God does not mean that all your questions will suddenly fade away, but it does bear witness to the shared experience that as you continue to walk this journey, you will learn to trust in God's promise beyond the immediate consequences. As Saint Augustine explained, we do not seek to understand in order to believe. We believe that we might understand. Faith simply opens the door of possibility for understanding. As Augustine put it, "Faith seeks, understanding finds."[9] When he was baptized, Augustine still had lingering questions about many matters of faith, but as he confessed his faith in God with the church, he gradually began to understand more about the faith the church confesses. His head and his heart learned to long for the One whose reality alone could stabilize his human restlessness. To put it differently, it is important to emphasize the *fides quae creditur* (the faith that is believed—i.e., the deposit of faith or knowledge of truth revealed in Christ) just as much as the *fides qua creditur* (the faith by which it is believed; i.e., personal faith or trusting obedience). Both are necessary.

But not everyone is so easily convinced. The story is told about an Orthodox priest giving a theological talk on the history of the creeds to a divinity school class. When the time came for questions at the end of the lecture, a student asked what to do if you find it impossible to affirm certain tenets of the creed. The priest answered that "you just say it," adding that "with a little practice and effort, most can learn it by heart." The student, apparently feeling misunderstood, asked a follow-up question: "What am I to do if I find I cannot affirm parts of the creed, like the Virgin Birth?" The priest gave the same answer, "You just stand with the congregation and say it. You keep saying it. Eventually it will come to you, with practice and time." At that point, the student felt that the priest had missed the point of the question entirely: "How can I say a creed that I do not believe?" The priest, now aware of the question, answered with clarity and wisdom: "It is not your creed, it is our creed. It may come to you, in time. For some, it takes longer than for others."[10]

As you have learned, the baptismal practice of our congregation is rooted in the believers' church tradition, which asks candidates to offer a personal confession of faith before being received into membership. This insistence on a confessional faith can be traced back to the old Puritan tradition that maintained the necessity that each church member must attest to what they called the "experience of grace." Reciting a creed is not considered a substitute for a personal confession of faith, which believers' churches contend goes all the way back to the days of the apostles. When asked by Jesus, "Who do you say that I am?" the apostle Peter answered, "You are the Messiah, the Son of the living God" (Matt 16:15–16). John the apostle records the personal confession from the mouth of the apostle Thomas, who, seeing the risen Christ, confessed, "My Lord and my God!" (John 20:28). And the apostle Paul made a personal confession of faith central when he declared, "If you confess with your lips that Jesus is Lord and believe in your heart that God raised him from the dead, you will be saved" (Rom 10:9). In the words of these apostolic witnesses, the experiential reality of primitive Christian faith given once and for all in Christ must be clearly attested by anyone seeking baptism.

Baptism is the door of the church, and the door of the church is open to all who come by faith in Jesus Christ. All who have faith in Christ are children of God (Gal 3:26). All who are baptized are united with Christ and with one another (Gal 3:27). All are invited to follow Christ, and none is excluded. All are welcome. And for those who follow by faith into the waters of baptism, "there is no longer Jew or Greek, there is no longer slave or free, there is no longer male and female; for all of you are one in Christ Jesus" (Gal 3:28). We are united in "one Lord, one faith, one baptism" (Eph 4:5). Yet the church has struggled to live into that reality. During the 1960s, our congregation wrestled with how to resist the powers of racial segregation and wondered what it might mean to be a church with a door that was open to all. The congregation changed its policy, but the struggle did not end with a vote. Hearts and minds, habits and practices, long under the sway of what the Bible calls "the spiritual forces of evil," are not so easily changed (Eph 6:12). As Jesus told the disciples, "This kind can come out only through prayer" (Mark 9:29). The great preacher and civil rights leader C. T. Vivian once prayed before a protest march, "Oh, God, we need you. Without you, we cannot make it because the battle is hard and the journey is long."[11] As you continue on your faith journey, you will discover that these powers of hatred, racism, and violence still threaten to close the door to full inclusion for all. You must continue the struggle to resist these powers.

The previous image from *The Pilgrim's Progress* shows Christian standing before the cross, where he believes and makes his confession of faith. It is a defining moment when the weight of his burden falls away, tumbles into a grave, and is never seen again. Yet learning to trust in God's full and complete forgiveness through Christ did not start or end there. As he began his journey with the help of Evangelist, Christian seemed conscious only of his burden. Then he entered through the wicket gate and came to Interpreter's house, where he was guided to a wall called *salvation* that led him to the cross.[12] At the cross, he confronted the reality that demanded he learn what it means to walk by faith (2 Cor 5:7). Learning to walk—not by what we see, but by what God has promised—takes faith. There are some who think that faith is only a personal experience: if anyone has faith in Christ, he or she is a new creation (2 Cor 5:17). They assume it is a simple transaction: I give God my faith, and God gives me salvation. What is missing in this version is any sense of how the faithfulness of Jesus Christ might have affected the rest of the world. The biblical witness presents the deliverance of God in Jesus Christ as the turning point of world history: "If anyone is in Christ, there is a whole new world!" This is good news: God has delivered creation from the destructive forces that would otherwise have determined humanity for ruin. The struggle for you will be to learn how to trust that what God has done in Christ has changed not only your life but the whole world.

Dorothy Day was a remarkable person who started a movement called the Catholic Worker. Her persistent witness for peace and justice was compelled by the vision of a world transformed through God's love in Christ, which is known and made known by showing hospitality to those at the margins of society. In her book *On Pilgrimage*, she wrote, "We must just live by faith, and the faith that God is good, that all times are in His hands." And she added, "I believe, Lord. Help Thou my unbelief."[13] She understood that our work as Christians is not to make the world come out right. God has already done that in the cross and resurrection of Jesus. But it takes faith to believe it. We must pray and not lose heart, asking God to increase our faith so we can live and love patiently, trusting that the world is being redeemed in Christ. When her biographer asked how she wanted to be remembered, she replied that she wanted her life to be "a living mystery" that "would not make sense if God did not exist."[14] Faith is the conviction to trust that the promised future toward which we move is in God's care and keeping. My prayer is that your faith might be increased to live a mysterious life that only makes sense because you believe in God.

Yours in the faith,

Interpreter

"Give me your hand." So he gave him his hand and he drew him out, and set him upon firm ground, and bade him go on his way.[1]

Principle 3

Baptism

Dear Pilgrim:

So far, I have discussed the basic teachings of Christ regarding repentance and faith. I now turn to the third principle commended by Hebrews: "instruction about baptisms" (Heb 6:2). As you can see, it speaks of baptism in the plural. You might be wondering why. The Bible actually speaks of baptism in three distinct ways. One is baptism by water. An example of water baptism is the story of the Ethiopian man who said to Philip as they were traveling through wilderness, "Look, here is water! What is to prevent me from being baptized?" (Acts 8:36). A second is baptism of the Spirit, which the risen Christ promised his followers (Acts 1:5). This spiritual sense of baptism can be seen at Pentecost when God's Spirit was poured out on and filled the Christians gathered in the upper room for prayer (Acts 2:1–4). Baptism is used in still a third way to describe full participation in the suffering and death of Christ. It is in this sense that Jesus, speaking of his suffering and death, asked James and John if they were able to be baptized with the baptism that he would be baptized in (Mark 10:38). It would be a mistake to think of these three as separate baptisms. There is only one baptism, but the

31

one baptism described in Ephesians 4:5 is part of the process of Christian initiation through which believers become members of the body of Christ.[2] The mystery of Christ's death and resurrection is linked with the gift of the Spirit, and participation in Christ's death and resurrection is linked with the reception of the Spirit. Baptism signifies and shares in both.[3]

This three-in-one way of speaking about baptism helps us begin to understand that there is more going on here than meets the eye. Baptism is a simple act that conceals a great mystery. The apostle Paul says that "in the one Spirit we were all baptized into one body" (1 Cor 12:13). This description suggests that every time someone is baptized in a gathered community, they join not only as a member of a local congregation but also as a member in the universal church, which includes all Christians around the world and throughout history. What this means is that all baptized Christians are one with each other in Christ and joined together into Christ's body, the church. It is simple yet mysterious. Baptism is not just a one-time event. It is a lifetime process. It is both an expression of faith and a means of grace. It is a sign of the pledged life of faith in Jesus Christ and a seal of the new life in the Holy Spirit. It is an ordinance of the gospel commanded by Christ and a sacrament that visibly signifies an invisible reality. It is a step toward ongoing discipleship and a witness to the new creation. It tells the story of the gospel that Christ has been crucified, buried, and raised, and it witnesses to the call of discipleship to die with Christ, to be buried into his suffering, and to live in a new way of life. No one can fully understand all this, but baptism is a commitment, as our catechism says, "to continue growing in the knowledge of what it means to be buried with Christ in a watery grave and raised to live in a new way of life."[4]

Jesus commanded his followers to "make disciples of all nations, baptizing them in the name of the Father and of the Son and of the Holy Spirit" (Matt 28:19). Baptism in the name of the Holy Trinity dates to the earliest Christian communities. In addition to the Gospel of Matthew, we find these instructions about baptism from an early Christian manual called the *Didache*: "Baptize as follows: after first explaining all these points, baptize in the name of the Father and of the Son and of the Holy Spirit, in running water. But if you have no running water, baptize in other water; and if you cannot in cold, then in warm. But if you have neither, pour water on the head three times in the name of the Father and of the Son and of the Holy Spirit."[5]

Through its history, the church has baptized with water by various means: still and running, cold and warm, dipping and pouring. Yet despite these differences in the method, all Christian baptism is to be performed in the name of the Trinity: the Father, the Son, and the Holy Spirit. Remembering our baptism, with Saint Patrick, we can then pray,

> I bind unto myself today
> the strong Name of the Trinity,
> by invocation of the same,
> the Three in One and One in Three.[6]

The practice in our denominational tradition is to immerse, or dip, as our forebears called it. Some have tried to suggest that our branch of the church goes all the way back to John the Baptist. As much as some might wish it were so, it is not. The earliest historical account of a baptistic Christian contending for baptism by immersion is Edward Barber's *A Small Treatise of Baptism or Dipping*, written in 1641. Barber began his tract with this declaration: "Thus it is clear, that the Lord Christ commanded his Apostles; and servants of the Gospel, first of all to teach, and thereby to gather Disciples: And afterward to dip those that were taught and instructed in the mysteries of the Gospel, upon the manifestation of their faith: which practice ought to continue to the end of the world."[7]

The issue was really less about how much water should be used in baptism and more about the need for those who are baptized to be committed followers of Jesus. Our church is not alone in this conviction. As I mentioned in a previous letter, the early Christian leader Tertullian recommended delaying baptism until the candidate is able to know Christ.[8] It is a wise practice because baptism is an important step in the faith journey that has profound implications.

Jesus said, "If any want to become my followers, let them deny themselves and take up their cross daily and follow me" (Luke 9:23). Immersion into the waters of baptism enacts the pledge of discipleship, to take up the cross and follow Jesus. At the center of what baptism is about is participation in the mystery into which Jesus was immersed through the suffering and death of the cross (Mark 10:38–39). His immersion into the deep waters of death is the reality Christian baptism signifies and the destiny all Christians are called to share in union with Christ (Rom 6:3). In baptism, we have died, and our lives are hidden with Christ in God (Col 3:3). As the seventeenth-century dissenter and exile Leonard Busher wrote, to be baptized is to be "dipped for dead in water."[9] Busher was not merely speaking about a symbolic death. He addressed these words to King James I of England, who had already shown his intolerance of religious dissenters by throwing them in prison and even sentencing them to death. When Jesus asked his followers James and John if they understood and were ready to be baptized into his death (Mark 10:38–39), they did not understand, but they soon did. James was executed by King

Herod Agrippa (Acts 12:1–2), and John reportedly survived being plunged in boiling oil and exiled to the island of Patmos, where he wrote the book of Revelation. None of us fully grasps the consequences of what it means to be baptized, but at some point, we too will face sacrifices that we did not choose. And when that time comes, we will understand more fully what it means that in baptism "we have been united with him in a death like his," but we will also learn the power of hope that "we will certainly be united with him in a resurrection like his" (Rom 6:5). For just as we "were buried with him in baptism, [we] were also raised with him through faith in the power of God, who raised him from the dead" (Col 2:12).

Baptism is about union with Christ, but it is also about rising up from the water to "walk in newness of life" (Rom 6:4). Jesus Christ—our great High Priest, who entered the deep waters of the grave and was raised into new life—commissions us in baptism to participate in the mission of the triune God. In baptism, we hear the words, as Jesus did, "You are my Son, the Beloved; with you I am well pleased" (Mark 1:11). The cleansing water reminds us that our sins have been washed away by Christ and we are renewed through the Holy Spirit (Titus 3:5; 1 Pet 3:21). Through baptism, you and I, along with every Christian, share in Christ's priestly ministry because in baptism, we are commissioned to carry out our priestly callings. So in baptism, we hear these words: "You are a chosen race, a royal priesthood, a holy nation, God's own people, in order that you may proclaim the mighty acts of him who called you out of darkness into his marvelous light" (1 Pet 2:9). As Martin Luther said, "All of us that have been baptized are equally priests. . . . Therefore we are all priests, as many of us as are Christians."[10] You have probably noticed that the Sunday worship bulletin for our church includes the motto "Every member a minister." We have a professional staff of ministers who are listed by name, but each of us is also a minister. Through baptism, we participate in the life of the triune God and are sent out to extend God's mission to the world.

In September 1785, William Carey, then a young and not yet ordained minister, asked a question: "Whether the command given to the apostles to 'teach all nations,' was not obligatory on all succeeding ministers to the end of the world, seeing that the accompanying promise was of equal extent." Carey's question implied an unusual interpretation of the Great Commission in Matthew 28:18–20 at the time, given that Protestants believed the office of apostle, to whom the commission was given, passed with the first generation of Christians. But he was not so easily convinced. In 1792, Carey published his missionary *Enquiry*, which took up the same question in great detail. In it, he argued that the commission of Jesus to "go into all the world, and preach the gospel to every creature" remains binding on all Christians, as evidenced by the fact that they continue to baptize, teach, and claim the promise of divine presence.[11] Carey soon traveled to India, where he spent the next forty-one years spreading the gospel until his death. It was eight years before Carey baptized his first Indian disciple, a man named Krishna Pal, but over seven hundred others eventually followed him into the waters of baptism.

When Carey and his family went to India, they were alone with few friends and fewer resources. It was not unlike the position of the apostles when Jesus commanded them to make disciples of all people and bring them under his rule. They went, not as a conquering army, but as a community of Christ-followers. Yet Jesus sent them out into the world with these final words: "Remember, I am with you always, to the end of the age" (Matt 28:20). The one who fulfilled the prophetic promise of Emmanuel, God with us (Matt 1:23), and who promised that when two or three are gathered in his name that he will be present (Matt 18:20), now promises to be with any and all who follow his commission unto the end of the world (Matt 28:20). We do not have to have it all figured out. If we practice the faith and follow the Master's plan, we can rest assured that the One who commands us to go will be with us every step of the way. So we pray again with Saint Patrick:

> Christ be with me, Christ within me,
> Christ behind me, Christ before me,
> Christ beside me, Christ to win me,
> Christ to comfort and restore me.[12]

The previous image from *The Pilgrim's Progress* shows Christian being lifted out of the Slough of Despond near the beginning of the story. Though it is not explicitly the scene of a Christian baptism, the imagery is certainly baptismal. Alone in the waters, Christian heard a voice. It was a man named Help who took Christian by the hand and lifted him out of the water and set him on the way.[13] Bunyan undoubtedly remembered his own baptism when John Gifford lifted him out of the Great Ouse River in Bedford. It brought to his mind the words of Psalm 40, which affirms,

> I waited patiently for the Lord;
>> he inclined to me and heard my cry.
> He drew me up from the desolate pit,
>> out of the miry bog,
> and set my feet upon a rock,
>> making my steps secure.
> He put a new song in my mouth,
>> a song of praise to our God.
> Many will see and fear,
>> and put their trust in the Lord.

Bunyan returns to baptismal imagery toward the end of the story, when Christian and Hopeful cross the River of

Death on their journey to the Celestial City, which lies just on the other side. As he made his way through the swelling current, Christian called out to his companion, "I sink in deep Waters, the Billows go over my head." But Hopeful called back, "Be of good cheer, my Brother, I feel the bottom, and it is good."[14]

The old hymn "How Firm a Foundation" reminds us that passing through the deep waters of baptism will be followed by more deep waters:

> When through the deep waters I call thee to go,
> The rivers of woe shall not thee overflow;
> For I will be with thee, thy troubles to bless,
> And sanctify to thee thy deepest distress.[15]

I wish I could tell you that when you enter into the waters of baptism, all that lies ahead is a lifetime of holy hallelujahs. But that would not be true. You will not wake up every morning with the thought that

> God's in His heaven—
> All's right with the world![16]

There will be days ahead when you will cry out in the words of the Psalmist, "Rescue me from sinking in the mire; let me be delivered from my enemies and from the deep waters. Do not let the flood sweep over me, or the deep swallow me up, or the Pit close its mouth over me" (Ps 69:14–15). But here is the good news: You are already dead. You are baptized! Your life is hidden with Christ in God. You have been buried with Christ into his death, and just as Christ was raised from the dead, so you too have been raised with him to walk in newness of life. Remember your baptism and be thankful!

Yours in deep waters,

Interpreter

PLATE 15 Christian Met by the Three Shining Ones

Now as he stood looking and weeping, behold three shining ones came to him, and saluted him, with "Peace be to you." So the first said to him, "Your sins are forgiven." The second stripped him of his rags, and clothed him with a change of clothes. The third also set a mark on his forehead, and gave him a roll with a seal on it, which he bid him look on as he ran, and that he should give it in at the Celestial Gate. So they went their way.[1]

Principle 4

Laying on of Hands

DEAR PILGRIM:

We now come to the fourth principle of basic Christian teaching—the laying on of hands. Although it may not be well known, it is actually a common practice in the Bible. For example, when Jacob prayed for God to bless his two grandsons, Ephraim and Manasseh, he laid his hands on them (Gen 48:14). The people of Israel consecrated the Levites by the laying on of hands (Num 8:10), and Moses designated Joshua as his successor by the laying on of hands (Num 27:18). Leviticus gives instructions for worshippers to lay their hands on the sacrifice before presenting it as an offering to the Lord (Lev 1:4). In each of these instances, the laying on of hands identifies who is the ritual object of God's action. Like pointing a finger, the imposition of hands says, "This one!"[2] It continued to be practiced by the early Christians as an act that invoked the bestowing of the Holy Spirit. For example, after a time of prayer, the church in Antioch discerned that they should dedicate Barnabas and Paul to spread the good news more widely. After the church had prayed, they laid hands on the apostles and sent them off as missionaries (Acts 13:2–3). When our congregation ordains deacons and pastors, there is a time for prayer and the laying on of hands, as we ask God to equip and empower these leaders with the gifts and graces for the ministry to which they have been called (1 Tim 4:14). So when the Letter to the Hebrews lists the laying on of hands as one of the basic teachings, it brings to mind this time-honored practice of prayer and consecration.

However, it is important to note that the laying on of hands in this list of basic principles immediately follows baptism, suggesting a particular context for the practice. It recalls the story in Acts when the apostles Peter and John traveled to Samaria to meet with a group of newly baptized followers of Jesus. After confirming their faith, the apostles prayed and laid hands on them, and these newly baptized believers received the Holy Spirit (Acts 8:14–17). The Samaritans had come to faith through the preaching of Philip, the very same Christian who led the Ethiopian man to faith and baptism on their desert journey (Acts 8:38). The story of the Samaritans does not suggest that there was anything unusual or flawed about their belief and baptism. Nor is there any indication that remarkable signs and wonders accompanied their reception of the Spirit. It simply suggests that baptism in water followed by the laying on of hands for the equipping of the Spirit is ordinary Christian practice. The third-century church leader Hippolytus described the practice of Christian baptism as followed by the laying on of hands and prayer.[3] Another third-century Christian leader, Tertullian, says that the anointing of oil, the imposition of hands, and the invocation of the Holy Spirit followed baptism.[4] Therefore, it seems that the laying on of hands following baptism in water in the name of the Father, the Son, and the Holy Spirit was a well-established tradition very early among Christians.

Even among the earliest Christians, establishing a definitive baptismal practice was not so easy. When the apostle Paul traveled on his third mission journey from Antioch, across the interior of Asia Minor, to Ephesus, he met a small group of "disciples." As they talked, it became apparent to Paul that something was lacking in the experience and deficient in the faith of these Ephesian believers. He suspected that they were not followers of Jesus but of some prophet, maybe even John the Baptist. Yet Paul did not criticize them. He simply inquired, "Did you receive the Holy Spirit when you became believers?" Their reply was odd: "No, we have not even heard that there is a Holy Spirit." Surely disciples of John would have known not only of the existence of the Holy Spirit but that the Holy Spirit would be poured out in the last days (Mark 1:8; Matt 3:11; Luke 3:16). Perhaps they were simply unaware that the end had come and that the awaited promise of God's Spirit had arrived. So Paul asked directly, "Into what then were you baptized?" They replied, "Into John's baptism." His suspicions now confirmed, Paul began to offer them instruction in the basic teaching of Christ. John's baptism was a baptism of repentance in preparation for the coming Messiah (Mark 1:4). These "disciples" were seekers of God's truth who had paused halfway on their journey. Their baptism and their faith were deficient and needed to be completed. So after hearing the gospel clearly stated, the halfway disciples in Ephesus were baptized upon the profession of their faith in Jesus. Then Paul laid hands on them and the Holy Spirit came upon them (Acts 19:1–6).

Baptism is a powerful practice when it is a sign of the pledged life of faith in Jesus Christ. The Ephesians undoubtedly knew about Christ, but they neither knew him nor had they been instructed in the basic teaching of Christ. When Paul explained that Jesus of Nazareth was Christ, they eagerly confessed their faith in him and were baptized in his name. Being baptized "in the name of the Lord Jesus" suggests that this baptism coincided with their confession of faith that

"Jesus is Lord" (Rom 10:9–10, 13). From the days of the earliest Christians, baptism was the occasion for one's confession of faith. When the Ethiopian eunuch asked Philip, "What prevents me from being baptized?" Philip answered, "If you believe with all your heart, you may." The Ethiopian replied, "I believe that Jesus Christ is the Son of God" (Acts 8:37 NASB). It is important to stress the connection between faith and baptism, but it is just as necessary to emphasize the bond between water and Spirit. Baptism is powerful practice because it is a sign of the pledged life of faith in Jesus Christ, but baptism is also a powerful practice because it is a seal of the new life in the Holy Spirit.

The story of the Ephesians in Acts 19 reminds us that baptism is not just something we do in obedience to the Lord's command. Baptism shares in something that God does. As part of baptism, Paul laid his hands on them, and "the Holy Spirit came upon them" (Acts 19:6). It stands as a witness to the connection between baptism and the reception of the Holy Spirit. This link between baptism and the Spirit is evident throughout the Book of Acts. Although there is no consistent pattern between all the accounts, whenever there is a baptism mentioned, the Holy Spirit is always present somewhere in the story. One of the clearest examples is the apostle Peter's sermon in Jerusalem at the Feast of Pentecost. When Peter finished his message, the crowd asked what they should do. He answered, "Repent, and be baptized every one of you in the name of Jesus Christ so that your sins may be forgiven; and you will receive the gift of the Holy Spirit" (Acts 2:38). It is important to notice that he did not say, "You may receive the gift of the Holy Spirit." He declared that if they would turn away from their sin and confess faith in Christ and be baptized, then they would receive the gift of the Holy Spirit. It is God's promise for everyone who calls on God's name.

The evidence that the Ephesian believers were filled with the Spirit was not that they spoke in tongues and prophesied (Acts 19:6). They were filled with the Spirit simply because they believed and were baptized. We know that the Spirit came upon them, not because there was an outward manifestation, but because of the promise of God that in baptism, "you will receive the gift of the Holy Spirit" (Acts 2:38). When we are baptized, we may not see the heavens part, or the Spirit descending like a dove, or the voice of God resounding from above, but when we are baptized in water, and the triune name is invoked, and hands are laid on our heads, and prayers are uplifted for blessing, the Holy Spirit is poured out on us. Whether we feel anything or not, baptism, accompanied by the confession of faith, prayer, and the laying on of hands, is a means of grace, through which the Spirit is freely given. This association between the practice of baptism and the coming of the Spirit is a clear indication that baptism is not a mere symbol or an empty memorial. It is not just an outward expression of an inward experience. Baptism belongs to the conversion of believers. If conversion is turning to God in Christ enabled by the Holy Spirit, then baptism is the embodiment, the completion, the seal of conversion.[5]

The laying on of hands as described in Acts and practiced by the early church was an integral dimension of baptismal practice. In early postapostolic Christian communities, converts were initiated into the church through baptism and the laying on of hands as part of a single rite, which was normally celebrated at Easter. Over time, the two acts of baptism and the laying on of hands evolved into separate and distinct sacramental rituals. The Catholic *Rite of Christian Initiation of Adults* retrieved elements of the ancient catechetical process in a unified rite, which includes the blessing of water, the renunciation of sin, the anointing with oil, the profession of faith, the baptism in water in the name of the Trinity, the clothing with the baptismal garment, and the laying on of hands, followed by the anointing with oil and the liturgy of the Eucharist.[6] Some Protestant churches have also begun to retrieve aspects of the ancient rituals of Christian initiation into their ceremonies of baptism and reception into membership. One even incorporates a fifth-century prayer accompanying the laying on of hands by the minister for the reception of the sevenfold gift of the Holy Spirit based on Isaiah 11:2.[7]

Other Protestants are somewhat more apprehensive about retrieving the laying on of hands at baptism because of its association with the practice of infant baptism and the rite of confirmation. A closer look at history tells a different story. Many of the early Baptists in England and America practiced the laying on of hands as part of baptism and reception into membership. Toward the end of the seventeenth century, two English-dissenting Protestant leaders, Thomas Grantham and Hercules Collins, both treated the laying on of hands following baptism in their catechisms as a universal principle of Christian teaching.[8] Among the early English Protestant dissenters, the strongest defense of the laying of hands on baptized believers for the reception of the Spirit was made by the London physician and preacher John Griffith. He argued that "in this ordinance of laying on of hands, we wait upon God, as babes in Christ, that we may receive the Holy Spirit to strengthen our weak souls, and to seal us for the day of redemption."[9] Unfortunately, Griffith was so adamant that the laying on of hands was a fundamental Christian precept, the General Baptists who followed his teaching refused to admit into membership baptized believers on whom no hands were laid.

But for others, the practice of the laying on of hands was a sign of continuity with the historic Christian church. The first

Association of Baptists in America recommended that the laying on of hands following baptism should be practiced "for a farther reception of the Spirit of promise, or for addition of the graces of the Spirit, and the influences thereof; to confirm, strengthen, and comfort them in Jesus Christ."[10] Morgan Edwards, an early minister of the First Baptist Church of Philadelphia, described the process of Christian initiation beginning with the confession of faith and baptism, followed by prayer and the laying on of hands, the offering of the right hand of fellowship and the kiss of charity.[11] All these actions have deep continuity with the baptismal practice of the early church. The current worship book of the Baptist Union of Great Britain commends a process of welcoming disciples into membership through the prayer for and the declaration of faith by candidates, baptism and the laying on of hands, making covenant promises and reception into membership, and the celebration of the Lord's Supper.[12] These examples suggest that our faith might be further strengthened by recovering the neglected practice of the laying on of hands after baptism, which emphasizes the gift of the Spirit.

The previous image from *The Pilgrim's Progress* shows Christian immediately after he came to the cross and his burden fell from his back. As he stood and wept, three messengers appeared and greeted him. The first pronounced his sins forgiven. The second gave him new clothing. The third put his hands on Christian's forehead and gave him a sealed scroll as a sign of his redemption that he would carry with him until the end of his earthly journey.[13] The awareness of forgiveness, the outward change, and the assurance of salvation are all part of evangelical experience, but they are all also enacted in the historic catechetical tradition of Christian initiation. Faith is a process, not an event, and the ritual practices that enact our faith signify the pilgrimage we are on.

So in baptism let us lift up our hearts and say, "Lord, increase our faith" (Luke 17:5), but let us also stretch out our hands and pray, "Lord, pour out your Spirit" (Acts 2:17–18). For as we rise from the water to join with Christ in God's mission to the world, we cannot follow this calling in our own strength. We can only do so to the extent that God empowers and equips us. As the prophet declared, it is "not by might, nor by power, but by my spirit, says the Lord of hosts" (Zech 4:6).

Yours in the Spirit,

Interpreter

Thus came Faithful to his end. Now I saw, that there stood behind the multitude a chariot and a couple of horses, waiting for Faithful, who (as soon as his adversaries had dispatched him) was taken up into it, and straightway was carried up through the clouds, with sound of trumpet, the nearest way to the Celestial Gate.[1]

Principle 5

Resurrection

Dear Pilgrim:

The fifth principle of the basic teaching of Christ is "the resurrection of the dead." The resurrection may be a core doctrine of the faith, but it is by no means an easy proposition to believe. In his book *Living Faith*, former US president Jimmy Carter tells about how as a nine-year-old boy, he was a member of a Sunday school class taught by his father. In that class, he received instruction in the basic teaching of the faith, including that Jesus was crucified and buried, that he was raised after three days, and that everyone who believes in him will also one day be raised from the dead. But the prospect of death and resurrection was troubling to young Carter, not so much because he could not fathom dead bodies coming back to life, but because he was terrified by the thought of being separated from his mother and father. By the age of twelve or thirteen, his anxiety grew so intense that at the end of every prayer, before saying "amen," he would add, "And, God, please help me believe in the resurrection." He felt ashamed that he had persistent doubts about what his pastor preached and his father taught, so outside of his prayers, he kept his questions to himself.[2]

Carter is not alone in his struggle to believe in resurrection. As you may recall, John's Gospel reports that on the third day after his crucifixion, Jesus appeared to his disciples. They communicated to Thomas, who was not with them, that they had seen the Lord and that he was alive. Thomas exclaimed he would not believe that Jesus had risen from the dead unless he could see and touch the Master's wounds. A week later, Jesus again appeared to his disciples. This time, Thomas was with them. Jesus invited Thomas to touch his nail-pierced hands and wounded side. Seeing Jesus in the flesh, alive, after he had died, was more than Thomas's doubts could withstand. He believed and confessed, "My Lord and my God!" To which Jesus replied, "Have you believed because you have seen me? Blessed are those who have not seen and yet have come to believe" (John 20:24–29).

Christians from the apostle Thomas to President Carter have acknowledged that it is hard to believe in resurrection when we cannot see it. Every time we attend a funeral, the dead are placed in a casket and lowered into a grave from which they do not return. Our uncertainty makes sense based on our experiences, though it also indicates that we lack the capacity to imagine what it might mean to believe in resurrection. Like the first disciples, our faith is mixed with doubt (Matt 28:17). Christian writer Frederick Buechner observed, "If you don't have doubts you're either kidding yourself or asleep." Some people fear doubts, but Buechner suggests they "are the ants in the pants of faith" that "keep it alive and moving."[3] I think he is right. Jesus told Thomas that it is possible to believe even when we have not seen and that those who believe without seeing are blessed. My colleague Stanley Hauerwas has a way of putting this: *"You can only act in the world you can see, and you can only come to see what you can say."*[4] There are times when we have trouble seeing the promise of resurrection clearly, not because we do not possess the mental capacity to understand or the will to believe. We cannot see because we lack the language to say what is going on. The good news is that the church gives us words to describe the convictions of our faith, and by learning that speech, we can then begin to see what we say. That language is the basic teaching of Christ. Learning this elemental grammar of the faith is essential to seeing what we say.

We become fluent in the language of the faith that enables us to see what we say by learning the story of the Bible, for "faith comes from what is heard, and what is heard comes through the word of Christ" (Rom 10:17). The Gospels and other books of the New Testament attest to the resurrection of Jesus of Nazareth and the promise of resurrection for those who believe in him. The biblical witness that Jesus was raised from the dead is not simply the suggestion that his mortal existence was quantitatively extended or that his immortal soul was freed from his mortal body. The resurrection of Jesus from the dead is not merely the resuscitation of his corpse. Nor is his resurrection just another way of saying that his body remained dead while his immortal soul lived on. The resurrection means that Jesus was lifted into a qualitatively different plane of existence. He was raised into eternal life, not because it would go on forever, but because it meant that in the resurrection, he shared fully and completely in the life of God. Moreover, the gospel declares that his experience is our hope (1 Cor 15:12–58). As Jesus promised, "Anyone who hears my word and believes him who sent me has eternal life, and does not come under judgment, but has passed from death to life" (John 5:24). We do not immediately see that, and yet we have been given a language to say it so that in learning to say it, we might begin to see it. In the words of the Apostles' Creed, we learn to see by saying, "We believe in the resurrection of the body."[5] We do not confess that "we understand the resurrection of the body." We believe it. We hope for it. We trust in the promise that in Christ, we have eternal life and have already passed from death to life.

The Bible also attests that all sons and daughters of earth shall die and return to the dust (Gen 2:17, 3:19). None shall escape, for "it is appointed for mortals to die" (Heb 9:27). Yet it does not take faith to believe in mortal existence—neither Jesus nor ours. We know that one day, death will come for us all. We do not know when, but we all know that we shall die. The Psalmist says:

> The days of our life are seventy years,
> or perhaps eighty, if we are strong;
> even then their span is only toil and trouble;
> they are soon gone, and we fly away (Ps 90:10).

There are people who live longer than seventy or eighty years. I have a friend who lived to be more than one hundred. But no one lives forever. No matter when death comes, it is final. Yet what makes death an enemy is not only that it means the cessation of personal existence. Death threatens life because it also terminates all social relations. Carter says that what animated his hope for eternal life was not the fear of his own death, or even the desire to live forever, but the realization that death would separate him from his parents. That anxiety about isolation and separation from the lives of those he loved most in the world moved him to hope against hope for the resurrection (Rom 4:18). As a mortal being, Jesus faced death, yet he passed from death to life, and his resurrection opened up an infinite set of relations that are sustained eternally in God's life.

Evangelical Christians from John Bunyan to Jimmy Carter have stressed conversion as the decisive moment in the faith journey. They emphasize that only by being "born again" (John 3:3 NASB) can we learn to say and see that in Christ, "there is a new creation," that "everything has become new" (2 Cor 5:17). They maintain that the moment of personal decision, when a person confesses Jesus Christ as Lord and Savior, is the determinative event of the Christian life. Only those who have "accepted Christ," they say, can be assured of claiming the promise of resurrection. As we have discussed, faith is one of the basic teachings. However, the Bible and Christian tradition point to the whole process of believing and being baptized as an appointed means for learning how to say and see the reconciling work of God in Jesus Christ. Upon the confession of faith in Jesus as Lord (Rom 10:9–10), we are lowered into a watery grave. When our bodies are dipped in the water, we are buried not as a sign of our own death but as a gesture to our participation in Christ's death. Baptism assures us not that we will die but that we are dead. We have died in Christ. We are buried into his death, we are raised from the dead with him (Rom 6:4), and our lives are hidden with Christ in God (Col 3:3). This dramatic enactment of God's deliverance in Jesus Christ is more than a turning point in our personal lives. It is the turning point of world history so that if anyone is in Christ, we see a completely new creation (2 Cor 5:17). We have been delivered from the destructive power of death to live freely and fully in the world made new through Jesus Christ the risen Lord.

The baptismal service of the early church was a dramatic and symbolic enactment of the passage from death to life. It began with prayer and fasting on Saturday night before Easter Sunday. Separated by gender, the candidates were instructed to take off their clothes to signify the passing away of the old to make way for the new creation in Christ (2 Cor 5:17). They were then brought into the baptistery chamber, where they turned to the west and renounced Satan. They then turned to the east and made a threefold confession of faith in the triune God, after which they descended into the water and were immersed three times in the name of the Father, the Son, and the Holy Spirit. Rising from the water, they were clothed in white robes, symbolic of attendants in wedding garments awaiting the coming of the bridegroom (Matt 25:1–10) and the marriage feast of the Lamb (Rev 19:6–10). The bishop would then lay hands on and pray for the newly baptized, anoint them with oil, administer the holy kiss to signify the coming of the Holy Spirit (John 20:22), and mark them with the sign of the cross to display their identity in Christ (1 Cor 1:21–22). Sometimes the baptized were given milk and honey to indicate their journey over Jordan into the Promised Land (Deut 31:20). The baptized were then salted on their tongues and given small lamps, recalling Jesus's words, "You are the salt of the earth. . . . You are the light of the world" (Matt 5:13–14). Hungry, tired, damp, and oily, they marched back to the sanctuary, singing the Easter hymn, "Christ is risen from the dead, he has crushed death by his death and bestowed life on those who lay in the tomb." As the bishop prayed, the bread and wine were spread out on the Lord's Table, and the newly baptized Christians were invited to partake in the Eucharistic meal.[6]

Such high drama leaves deep impressions on bodies and minds enabling the remembrance of baptism. As former Archbishop of Canterbury Rowan Williams observed, baptism "imprints upon the believer the mark of Easter."[7] The third-century Christian Tertullian stated it even more strongly when he declared, "Flesh is the very condition on which salvation hinges."[8] This is why, he says, our flesh is washed in water, anointed with oil, signed with the cross, shadowed with the imposition of hands so that the soul may be cleansed, consecrated, fortified, and illuminated. "And so," Tertullian concluded, having been baptized, we know in our bodies that "the flesh shall rise again."[9] It should not be surprising, then, that when Martin Luther's students asked him about his assurance of salvation, he simply said, "I am baptized." "God," he explained, "could not have given me better security of my salvation, and of the gospel, than by the death and passion of his only Son: when I believe that he overcame death," adding "when I have the seal of baptism . . . I am well provided for."[10] To remember our baptism is to know, as our catechism says, that "in life, in death, in life beyond death, I belong to my faithful Savior, and nothing can separate me from God's love" (Rom 8:31–39; 1 Cor 15:54–56).[11]

Dietrich Bonhoeffer was a Christian pastor and theologian in Germany. He was imprisoned during the Second World War because of his resistance to Hitler and the Nazis. Sensing that his death was near, he wrote to his close friend Eberhard Bethge from his prison cell: "It is only when one loves life and the earth so much that without them everything seems to be over that one may believe in the resurrection and a new world."[12] Believing in the resurrection is not a denial of this world. Yet, as Bonhoeffer well understood, the call of discipleship means taking up the cross and following Jesus. It is a "call to abandon the attachments of this world." "As we embark upon discipleship," Bonhoeffer wrote, "we surrender ourselves to Christ in union with his death—we give over our lives to death." For "when Christ calls [us], he bids [us] come and die."[13] And because in baptism we have been buried into Christ's death and raised with him into eternal life, we know in our bodies "that neither death, nor life, nor angels, nor rulers, nor things present, nor things to come, nor powers, nor height, nor depth, nor anything else in all creation, will be able to separate us from the love of God in Christ Jesus our Lord" (Rom 8:38–39).

The image at the beginning of the chapter depicts the death of Christian's fellow pilgrim Faithful, who was imprisoned and executed for his faith by the citizens of Vanity Fair. Yet God, the One who overrules all things, reversed their judgment and vindicated Faithful, taking him up in a whirlwind and carrying him away in a chariot of fire straight to the Celestial City (2 Kgs 2:11).[14] In death, Faithful becomes a model of discipleship, as one who takes up the cross and follows Jesus. Bunyan's story brings to mind another story from the Bible: when three young men refused to yield to the demand of Nebuchadnezzar, king of Babylon, saying, "If our God whom we serve is able to deliver us from the furnace of blazing fire and out of your hand, O king, let him deliver us. But if not, be it known to you, O king, that we will not serve your gods and we will not worship the golden statue that you have set up" (Dan 3:17–18).

Throughout the centuries, this story has been read by pilgrims who realized that they were not going to be delivered from their troubles in this world. They knew that very likely they would be thrown into the furnace and that they would not emerge from the flames unharmed. Yet they faced their troubles, trusting in the One who is able to deliver, but even if not, they were still committed to trust in life, in death, in life beyond death. The words of the hymn say it well:

> When through fiery trials thy pathway shall lie,
> My grace, all-sufficient, shall be thy supply.
> The flame shall not hurt thee; I only design
> Thy dross to consume, and thy gold to refine.[15]

Dutch Mennonites gathered accounts of Christians who were faithful unto death in a book called *Martyrs Mirror*. It tells about people being burned and drowned, having gunpowder put in their hair and set on fire, having their witness silenced with tongue screws, and much more. One story in particular stands out. It is about a man named Dirk Willems who was arrested and jailed in 1569 in Asperen, Holland, for the crime of believer baptism. One night he slipped out of his cell and was pursued by an authority of the state. It was in the middle of winter, and Willems escaped by crossing over the river, which was frozen. His lone pursuer followed him across the ice but broke through and fell into frigid water. Rather than continuing on, Willems turned back and pulled the man out, thus saving the man's life but forfeiting his own. So it happened that Willems was imprisoned, tried, and executed.[16] Mennonite grandmothers tell this story to their grandchildren before being baptized. I think it might be worth telling to all those who venture into the dangerous waters that unite us with Christ's suffering and death and out of which we are raised to live in the new life of his resurrection.

Let us then pray: We will trust you, O God most high, for you are able to deliver us. But even if not, we will trust you still until our final breaths. Amen.

Yours in that hope,

Interpreter

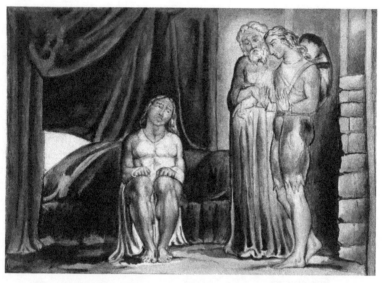

Why, I thought that the day of Judgement was come, and that I was not ready for it. But this frightened me most, that the angels gathered up several, and left me behind. Also the pit of hell opened her mouth just where I stood. My conscience too afflicted me; and as I thought, the Judge had always his eye upon me, showing indignation in his countenance.[1]

Principle 6

Eternal Judgment

Dear Pilgrim:

We now come to the sixth and final principle of basic Christian teaching: eternal judgment. The Bible speaks of a time at the end of history when God will render final judgment on the living and the dead. It is sometimes called "Judgment Day," "the day of wrath," or "the day of the Lord." The prophets often described it with harsh images, comparing God's wrath to a consuming fire that will be poured out on the wicked (Heb 12:29). Religious people too often wrongly assume that God's judgment will be poured out on their enemies while they themselves will be vindicated and rewarded. But as the prophet Amos warned the people of Israel, the coming day of the Lord will be darkness rather than light (Amos 5:18). When John the Baptist appeared in the wilderness of Judea, he called the people to repent before the coming day of judgment, when God "will gather his wheat into the granary; but the chaff he will burn with unquenchable fire" (Matt 3:12). The book of Revelation offers a frightening vision of final judgment, when from a great white throne, God decrees that those whose names are not found in the book of life must be thrown into a lake of fire (Rev 20:11–15). The Bible is filled

with terrifying descriptions of final judgment, which has led many believers to suppose that these visions are literal previews of the life beyond.

Henry Jessey was a dissenting Protestant minister who wrote a catechism for his London congregation in 1652. It asks, "What must be our condition after death, when God sends Jesus Christ to judgment?" The prescribed answer states, "Naughty ones, in the naughty way, for their naughtiness, must be in hell forever. Good ones, in the good way, by the grace of our Lord Jesus Christ, must be in heaven forever (Matt 25:46)."[2] It is a frightening thought, and it raises the question if there is any escape from eternal judgment. Are we not all naughty? Writing not long after Jessey, John Bunyan described how Interpreter led Christian into a room where they met a man trembling after awaking from a dream about Judgment Day. In his dream, he saw a human figure on a cloud, like the Son of Man described in Daniel, chapter 7, calling for the book of life to be opened. From his heavenly throne, the eternal Judge kept watch over every deed, "including every secret thing, whether good or evil" (Eccl 12:14). And the trembling man confessed to Christian that his conscience brought to mind his sins, afflicting and accusing him on every side (Rom 2:15–16). As Christian reflects on what he has seen, Interpreter reminds him that the Comforter (John 14:26) will guide him on his journey, which leads him immediately to the cross, where his burden is loosed from his back and he is freed to live by the mercy of God.[3]

The so-called hellfire and brimstone sermon, popularized by American evangelical preachers, drew deeply from these biblical images to appeal to the emotions, especially fear, as a motivation for the conversion of sinners. Perhaps the most famous of these sermons is Jonathan Edwards's "Sinners in the Hands of an Angry God," preached July 8, 1741, in Enfield,

Connecticut. Its vivid visualizations of the horrors of hell have captured the imagination of readers through the years. Edwards warned, "There is the dreadful pit of the glowing flames of the wrath of God; there is hell's wide gaping mouth open; and you have nothing to stand upon, nor anything to take hold of: there is nothing between you and hell but the air; 'tis only the power and mere pleasure of God that holds you up."[4]

"You hang by a slender thread," Edwards continued, "with the flames of divine wrath flashing about it, and ready every moment to singe it, and burn it asunder." However, as he told his listeners, God's wrath is not the end of the story. The last word is mercy, for only God's love can spare us from the torments of hell: "You have . . . nothing to lay hold of to save yourself, nothing to keep off the flames of wrath, nothing of your own, nothing that you ever have done, nothing that you can do, to induce God to spare you one moment." Yet God has mercifully extended favor to all who will only repent and turn to Christ for help.[5]

But it was not only Old and New England puritan preachers who drew on images of hellfire and damnation to imagine eternal judgment. James Weldon Johnson shows how the sermons of black preachers in the American South narrated the biblical images of judgment. In the opening prayer of *God's Trombones*, the preacher begs, "Lord, have mercy on proud and dying sinners—Sinners hanging over the mouth of hell." And he adds, "Ride by the dingy gates of hell, and stop poor sinners in their headlong plunge."[6] It is a reminder, as Frederick Buechner observed, that "the gospel is bad news before it is good news."[7] All have sinned (Rom 3:23), and the wages for sin is death (Rom 6:23). In Johnson's last sermon, which is a description of Judgment Day, the preacher begins,

In that great day,
People, in that great day,

> God's a-going to rain down fire.
> God's a-going to sit in the middle of the air
> To judge the quick and the dead.

Yet the preacher warns the unrepentant:

> Too late, sinner! Too late!
> Good-bye, sinner! Good-bye!
> In hell, sinner! In hell!
> Beyond the reach of the love of God.[8]

Is there really a place that is forever beyond the reach of God's love? It is a question worth asking. By the twentieth century, plenty of ministers and theologians had concluded that notions of divine wrath and eternal judgment were not fitting matters for Christian faith and proclamation. They maintained that to suggest we are "sinners in the hands of an angry God" is an inappropriate, perhaps even abusive, use of religious language based on a crude, literal sense of biblical imagery. Yet this modern aversion to divine wrath seemed to lead to a sentimental view of God who was far too nice to damn anyone to hell for eternity. One theologian observed that the revisionists preached a gospel that explained how "a God without wrath brought [humans] without sin into a kingdom without judgment through the ministrations of a Christ without a cross."[9] My theological mentor Jim McClendon thought that biblical images of the last judgment are examples of what he called "picture-thinking."[10] These futuristic images of heaven and hell are not meant to be taken as straightforward, ordinary objects of belief. What it means, then, to believe in last judgment is to act in such a way that this picture is before our minds. To believe it is to grasp it so that we not only change our views. We change our lives. These pictures warn us not to neglect the great gift of salvation in Christ, and they show us that our actions in response have ultimate consequences. That seems right to me.

Something else I learned from Jim is that eternal judgment is not only about the things that come last on the final day "when the faith shall be sight" and "the clouds be roll'd back as a scroll." It is also about the things that last in the here and now.[11] One of the most striking biblical pictures of final judgment is Jesus's parable about ten young women (Matt 25:1–13). All were invited to participate as torchbearers for the procession in a wedding party. Five brought extra oil for their lamps, and five did not. When the bridegroom did not come as they expected, they all fell asleep. They were awakened at midnight by an announcement that the bridegroom was coming. All of them jumped up and began trimming their wicks. The five who came prepared added oil to their lamps. Those who brought no oil asked to borrow some, but they were told that there was not enough to share. So they left to buy oil for their lamps. Arriving late to the banquet and finding the door shut, the five bridesmaids cried out to the bridegroom, "Lord, Lord, open to us!" But he answered them, "I do not know you." Hellfire-and-damnation preachers have read these words to mean,

> Too late, sinner! Too late!
> In hell, sinner! In hell!

Then we remember that eternal judgment is not only about things that come last. It is also about things that last. Keeping the picture of the closed door before our minds might mean something very different than hellfire and damnation in the end. It may force us to recognize that we must live each day in such a way that when crises come, we are ready. The oil we need to illuminate our ways in the darkness cannot be borrowed. We cannot say to our friends and neighbors, "May I have a little of your peace of mind?" or "Could you share your faithfulness with me?" or "Would you please lend me a wee bit of your joy?"

or "Can I borrow some of your good marriage?" Just as the foolish bridesmaids could not borrow oil for their lamps, so moral character is not shareable either. We are formed in the virtues that sustain us in life and death by keeping pictures of eternal judgment before our minds so that they change not just our views about what comes last but our lives in ways that last.

In the parable of the sheep and goats, Jesus gives us insight into how a picture of eternal judgment changes our lives in lasting ways. When it comes time for judgment to be passed, the Son of Man, to whom all desires are known and no secrets are hidden, will render judgment based on the treatment of the hungry, the thirsty, the stranger, the naked, the sick, and the prisoner, who he called "the least of these" (Matt 25:31–46). His judgment is based on the way these sheep and goats behave when they could not begin to imagine it counted. Their actions when they thought no one was watching are precisely what counts because they show who they really are. Their uncalculating love, their aimless faithfulness, or their lack thereof, reveals their destinies. Yet the parable suggests it is an even bigger mistake to assume that eternal judgment is all about us. It really is not about us at all. It is about Jesus—crucified, risen, and returning—Son of God and Son of Man. He is the judge. In identifying with "the least of these," he embodies the way of the kingdom that will endure when all else will pass away. The deeds that unconsciously display our true characters ultimately matter, not because they are about us, but because they reflect the character of the One, as the ancient hymn attests,

> who, though he was in the form of God,
>> did not regard equality with God
>> as something to be exploited,
> but emptied himself,
>> taking the form of a slave,
>> being born in human likeness

And being found in human form,
> he humbled himself
> and became obedient to the point of death—
> even death on a cross (Phil 2:6–8).

And only when we see that this is about him, the Servant King, can we begin to imagine what the apostle Paul might have meant when he wrote, "Let the same mind be in you that was in Christ Jesus" (Phil 2:5).

Where the pictures of judgment in the Synoptic Gospels of Matthew, Mark, and Luke focus on Christ coming as the Son of Man at the end of time to judge the world, the images of judgment from the Gospel of John show Jesus Christ in his earthly ministry as the agent of divine judgment. The vision of judgment in the Synoptics is futuristic, and the picture of judgment in John is already realized. One shows us pictures of the things that are not yet, and the other displays a vision of the things that have already come to pass. The aim of Christ as Judge in the Gospel of John is not punishment and retribution but redemption and reconciliation. The word of God's judgment in Christ is love incarnate. Whoever receives God's loving gift will not perish but will be granted eternal life (John 3:16). For God sent the Son as Judge, not to condemn, but to save (John 3:17). Yet there is no need to wait until the end of time for this judgment. The light that shines in Jesus Christ is the life of the world (John 1:4–5). Those who believe in him are made members of God's family (John 1:10–11). They are baptized, born from above, of water and Spirit (John 3:5). Those who believe in him are not condemned, but those who refuse to believe are condemned already (John 3:18). God's judgment is to send the light of love in Jesus the Christ (John 3:19). Those who believe in the Son have eternal life, but those who reject the Son will not see life but will endure God's wrath (John 3:36). Whatever wrath is, it is surely the willful rejection of love. Whoever rejects the word of God's incarnate love in Jesus Christ already has received the final judgment (John 3:36).

Things eternal come last, but things are eternal because they last. Perhaps the simplest description of what lasts is Saint Paul's statement, "Love never ends" (1 Cor 13:8). It is why the Scottish minister and theologian Henry Drummond called love "the greatest thing in the world." Drummond is unequivocal: "Where love is, God is. He that dwells in love dwells in God. God is love. Therefore love. Without distinction, without calculation, without procrastination, love."[12] When all else fails, love endures, and it lasts because it is eternal. It never ends—ever. The word of love, spoken from eternity, became incarnate in Jesus Christ. That is why love is the final and enduring word of God. As Drummond observed,

> Love must be eternal. It is what God is. On the last analysis, then, love is life. Love never fails, and life never fails, so long as there is love. The reason why in the nature of things love should be the supreme thing—because it is going to last; because in the nature of things it is an eternal life. It is a thing that we are living now, not that we get when we die; that we shall have a poor chance of getting when we die unless we are living now.[13]

Jesus Christ was love incarnate, but in becoming human, the glory of divine love lay hidden within the veil of human flesh. In Christ, God identified with humanity. Yet humanity did not recognize eternal love in him (John 1:10–11). All humanity cried out in one voice with the crowd in Jerusalem, "Crucify him!" (Mark 15:13), but all humanity has been acquitted and released along with the criminal Barabbas while Jesus was condemned and crucified (Mark 15:6–15). Though he never sinned, he endured the consequence of sin for us (2 Cor 5:21). The judgment of history—as represented by religious and civil authorities, by opponents and adversaries, and even by his friends and followers—was death. He accepted that judgment, refusing to defend himself and embodying forgiveness for all, even for his enemies. Yet death was not the final word, as God the Father reversed history's judgment, raising Jesus by the Spirit into eternal life and declaring him Son. In Christ, God has spoken both a life-giving yes to the world and a death-dealing no to sin and evil. On the cross, Jesus bore the no for all so that in his resurrection, all that remains is God's yes (2 Cor 1:19–20; John 3:17, 5:24). The cross and resurrection thus reveal that God's judgment for the world is love (Rom 5:8).

In the opening scene of Bunyan's *The Pilgrim's Progress*, when Christian began his journey, he opened the Bible and beheld visions of last judgment. In distress, he cried out, "What must I do to be saved?"[14] When Evangelist appeared, Christian continued, "I am condemned to die, and after that to come to judgment" (Heb 9:27). Evangelist directed him to "flee from the wrath to come" (Matt 3:7). When he arrived at Interpreter's house, Christian met the man afraid of the day of judgment. Neither of these scenes is contrary to the biblical descriptions of eternal judgment. However, as I have suggested, these types of readings fail to grasp the meaning of the power of these pictures of judgment in the Bible to shape our lives in the ways of love, which in the end is all that lasts. When we say that we believe in eternal judgment, it means that we keep this picture before us so that it will enable us to live into the love that not only comes last but also lasts.

I want to close this letter by directing you to another picture of eternal judgment, painted by Matthias Grünewald in his magnificent *Isenheim Altarpiece*. The central image shows John the Baptist with his hand outstretched pointing to Jesus on the cross. It is an unnatural image. The finger of John's hand is enlarged and out of proportion to the rest of the figures, as if to say in an exaggerated and amplified voice, "In this man, love bore our transgressions, and in this man, love was raised up into life eternal." Above the desk where Karl Barth wrote his magisterial *Church Dogmatics*, there hung a copy of Grünewald's picture. It kept the image of God's judgment always before his mind as he wrote. It reminded him that in Christ, love was condemned and judged by the world and that in Christ, love was vindicated and elevated. Most of all, it kept his focus on God, whose nature and name are love. Upon confessing our faith in Christ in baptism we are buried with him into the no and raised into the yes.[15] Singer-songwriter John Prine said it with clarity and simplicity:

> If by chance I should find myself at risk,
> A-falling from this jagged cliff,
> I look below, and I look above;
> I'm surrounded by your boundless love.[16]

As Pope Francis has said, "The name of God is mercy."[17] Remember your baptism, and be thankful that your life is surrounded by God's boundless love, unbounded even by time because love never ends (1 Cor 13:8).

Yours in love,
Interpreter

Now I saw in my dream that when Christian and Hopeful went in at Heaven's Gate they were transfigured and clothed in robes that shone like gold. There they were met by bright hosts who came with harps and crowns: Then I heard in my dream that all the bells in the City rang for joy and that it was said unto them, "Enter ye into the joy of your Lord." And after that the gates were once again shut, which when I had seen, I wished myself among them. Then I awoke, and behold it was a dream.[1]

Now I saw in my dream that when Christian and Hopeful went in at Heaven's Gate they were transfigured and clothed in robes that shone like gold. There they were met by bright hosts who came with harps and crowns: Then I heard in my dream that all the bells in the City rang for joy and that it was said unto them, "Enter ye into the joy of your Lord." And after that the gates were once again shut, which when I had seen, I wished myself among them. Then I awoke, and behold it was a dream.[1]

Conclusion

Going on toward Perfection

Dear Pilgrim:

We have come to our last conversation on the basic teaching of Christ, but it is only the beginning of the faith journey. The six principles we have discussed are foundational because they rest on the foundation that has been laid once for all in Jesus Christ (1 Cor 3:11). They are not so much fences designed to restrain our faith. Instead, they are more like guideposts meant to give us direction in the Christian journey from beginning to end. Over the centuries, instruction in these elemental matters has been critical to ensuring that the faith is faithfully handed on to faithful followers of Christ (2 Tim 2:2). Although once common among most churches, catechetical instruction has become an almost forgotten practice. Regrettably, the basic religious formation many young people get today comes down to thinking that God is nice and that we should be nice too.[2] Grasping the basic teaching of Christ is crucial for beginning the faith journey, but we have to keep going. The author of the Letter to the Hebrews wrote to believers who were stuck. They had received instruction in the basic teaching of Christ, but they had not grown in the faith. They should have moved on to a more substantial diet, but they were still like infants living on spiritual pabulum. When believers become stuck in the faith journey, they lack the power of moral discernment necessary to become mature followers of Christ (Heb 5:12–14). They need to learn how to get unstuck and go on to perfection (Heb 6:1).

The appeal to go on toward perfection can be seriously misunderstood. It does not mean that the aim of the Christian life is a state of sinless perfection—but to dismiss the call to perfection as an impossible goal is equally problematic. John Wesley, the founder of the Methodist movement, emphasized that going on to perfection is rooted in the desire to live more fully into the love of God.[3] As you remember from my previous letter, living into love is not only moving toward what comes last at the end of the journey. It is being formed into what lasts eternally because love never ends (1 Cor 13:8). One way to describe the fullness of God's love that awaits us and endures forever is "the perfect" (1 Cor 13:10 NASB). Methodist elders must still answer the question at ordination: Are you going on to perfection? They must be prepared to respond: Yes, by the grace of God.[4] What does it mean to go on to perfection? Wesley and the Methodists rightly point to the importance of ongoing growth in love as essential to Christian maturity. They stress that we have been saved by grace and we are being saved by grace. It reminds me of a story about a new believer who asked a more mature Christian if conversion was the end of the Christian life. The older Christian answered, "Yes, it is the front end." Yet far too many baptized Christians are stuck at the beginning of the faith journey without a commitment to go on. The Swiss Reformed theologian Emil Brunner warned that the failure to go on was rooted in a deficient baptismal practice. He asked, "What does the fact of having been baptized mean for a large number of contemporary people who do not know and do not even care to know whether they have been baptized?"[5]

The appeal to go on toward perfection underscores the basic truth that the Christian life requires development toward maturity. Just as we grow up physically and socially, so we are made to grow up spiritually. Something has gone wrong if we have the same faith at age thirty-five or sixty-five that we had at age fifteen. It is important to gain an elementary knowledge of the faith, but we have to continue growing so that we become mature followers of Christ. In baptism, we have been raised up with Christ and our lives are hidden with Christ in God. We have put off the old and put on the new, but we must clothe ourselves in love, "which binds everything together in perfect harmony" (Col 3:1–14). Growing into a fuller and deeper understanding of what it means to love God and our neighbors is the tie that binds so that everything fits, giving life integrity and wholeness. However, there is more to perfection than becoming mature and whole. Jesus said that anyone who desires to follow him must "be perfect as [our] Father in heaven is perfect" (Matt 5:48 GW). Jesus was not suggesting that we could be God. No one except God can be God. He was saying we could be like God, who is always perfectly God. It is God's nature to be God, and it is our nature to become who we really are and who we are meant to be. To seek perfection means being discontent with simply being who we happen to be as we are and asking who we could be if we realized our true nature in Christ's new creation.[6] God made us to move toward that end. It is who we are, and baptism signifies the journey into that identity. Coming to an understanding of our true nature, in the language of the *Westminster Confession*, is seeing that our end is to glorify and enjoy God now and forever.[7] Going on toward perfection then is seeking to fulfill our nature and reach our purpose in life.

During the course of these conversations, we have turned our attention often to John Bunyan's story *The Pilgrim's Progress*.

Its narrative displays faith not as a one-time experience but as a lifelong journey. The theme of pilgrimage permeated the literature and culture in medieval and early modern England. One of the most well-known examples is *The Canterbury Tales*, which recounts stories told by a group of pilgrims traveling from London to Canterbury to visit the shrine of Thomas Becket. Yet dissenting Christians like Bunyan were more favorably disposed to books like *The Plain Man's Pathway to Heaven*, which offered a theological account of the Christian journey in the format of a dialogue between characters.[8] However, the primary source of inspiration for Bunyan was the biblical description of the faithful, who "were strangers and pilgrims on the earth" (Heb 11:13).[9] Bunyan's story stands in the dissenting tradition of the Lollard Christian Sir John Oldcastle, who, in 1413, asserted that "every man dwelling on earth is a pilgrim, either towards bliss or else towards pain."[10]

Pilgrimage for Bunyan was not so much a matter of geography as it was theology. *The Pilgrim's Progress* is not the story of a journey by travelers through cartographic space. It is an account of the odyssey of the soul in a spiritual reality. It tells the story of every Christian. Pausing in his journey, Christian stopped at Interpreter's house for instruction in the basic teaching of Christ, but he continued on the way, which did not end until he crossed the River of Death and passed into the Celestial City. Bunyan's narrative reflects an account in early Christianity expressed by Saint Augustine, who described the Christian life as a pilgrimage and the church as a pilgrim community of resident aliens. It echoes the language of the apostle Paul, who suggested that the church on earth is a colony of heaven (Phil 1:27) and the citizenship of its members is in heaven (Phil 3:20). For Augustine, the church is in part a pilgrim community and in part a community abiding in heaven. Christians in their earthly pilgrimage are resident aliens yearning for home. They are exiles like the Jews in Babylon. They are refugees like Roman citizens displaced in North Africa. Christian pilgrims are homesick. Their hearts are heavy. They travel homeward, walking by faith, living in hope, and soaring on the wings of love.[11]

One of the earliest written accounts of Christian pilgrimage is the story of a young woman named Egeria who traveled from her home in Spain to the Holy Land in the fourth century. She visited places associated with biblical figures and events, but she was most interested in visiting the church in Jerusalem and experiencing its worship and liturgy. When she arrived in Jerusalem, the bishop was the elderly Cyril, who more than three decades earlier had first delivered his celebrated *Catechetical Lectures*. Egeria describes the baptism and initiation process in the Jerusalem Church, which included three hours of catechesis each day during Lent and culminated with baptism on Easter followed by a week of instruction in the mysteries for the newly baptized.[12] Where baptismal catechesis focuses on biblical and doctrinal instruction, the purpose of mystagogical instruction is to explain to newly baptized Christians the spiritual significance of baptism, anointing, Eucharist, and liturgy.[13] Baptism signifies putting off the old nature and putting on the new nature in Christ (Gal 3:27). Through water and Spirit, we are born anew (John 3:3–7), but we must not remain as infants, living on milk. We must become mature and growing followers of Christ, nourished and sustained by spiritual food (Heb 5:12–14).

God entrusts us with holy mysteries to strengthen us for the journey. These gifts belong to all God's people, but by receiving instruction in the mysteries, we become stewards (1 Cor 4:1). Within the ordinary figures of water and oil, bread and wine, words and gestures, the deep mysteries of the faith lie hidden in plain view. They are mysteries because there is more going on here than meets the eye, but they become available only to those who believe. In a lecture to a group of catechumens, Saint Augustine explained that "these realities are called sacraments (or mysteries) because in them one thing is seen, while another is grasped. What is seen is a mere physical likeness; what is grasped bears spiritual fruit."[14] With the whole church, we must hold these mysteries in trust. They are bread for our journeys. Without them, we grow weak and weary in the faith. So we pray, Abba, Father, "give us this day our daily bread" (Matt 6:11). We remember that as Israel "had the manna to nourish them in the wilderness to Canaan; so have we the sacraments, to nourish us in the church, and in our wilderness-condition."[15] These holy mysteries are life-giving sustenance for us. They are the sources of healing, strength, and nourishment as we walk by faith and not by sight (2 Cor 5:7).

No pilgrim will last long on the journey without the life-giving sustenance of God's holy manna, but there is one more item you will need to take with you—the Bible. Jesus told his followers, "If you continue in my word, you are truly my disciples; and you will know the truth, and the truth will make you free" (John 8:31–32). One way that Christians have continued in the word is through the practice of continuous reading, or *lectio continua*. That does not mean reading nonstop, twenty-four hours a day, seven days a week. It names a historic practice of reading whole books of Scripture in sequence daily or on Sundays. I remember as a young person being challenged to read the whole Bible in a year. More than once I got bogged down and stopped somewhere in the books of Leviticus or Chronicles, but over time, as I made it further through, I realized that I was gaining a sense of the scope of the entire biblical story. One of the passages that particularly stood out to me was a prayer by the Psalmist:

How can young people keep their way pure?
>   By guarding it according to your word.
With my whole heart I seek you;
>   do not let me stray from your commandments.
I treasure your word in my heart,
>   so that I may not sin against you (Ps 119:9–11).

That prayer gives us the voice to say that it is worth attending to God's word with our whole hearts. More importantly, praying those words cultivates the desire to be like the Beroean Christians who "received the word with all eagerness, examining the Scriptures daily to see if these things were so" (Acts 17:11 ESV).

In looking back, I can see how important the Bible has been for keeping me on the path in this journey of faith. As you embark on the pilgrim way, I encourage you to keep God's word with you. It will be a lamp for your feet and a light to your path (Ps 119:105). Receiving light from the word is a long-held source of strength for Christian pilgrims. Before the Pilgrim Church set sail on the Mayflower from Holland to Plymouth, John Robinson delivered one final sermon. He reminded them of their "covenant with God and one with another, to receive whatsoever light or truth shall be made known to us from God's written Word." Then he charged them to be open as they continued the journey because "he was very confident the Lord had more truth and light yet to break forth out of his holy Word."[16] It is a reminder to us that the Christian life is a quest of unfolding truth. With the Bible in our hands, let us walk together in the ways made known as we are led by the Spirit to ways yet to be known.

Last year, two of our close friends walked the Camino de Santiago, the Way of Saint James, from southern France over the Pyrenees and across northern Spain to Cape Finisterre on the Atlantic coast, which the Romans called the "end of the earth." The Camino is an ancient pilgrimage of over five hundred miles that ends at the Cathedral of Santiago de Compostela in northwest Spain, where the body of James the apostle was reportedly taken from Jerusalem after his martyrdom in 44 CE (Acts 12:1–2). The Camino was one of the most popular routes for Christian pilgrims during the middle ages, but by the late twentieth century, only a few hundred registered pilgrims made the journey annually. There has been a revival of interest in the Camino that has led to a growing number of people returning to this ancient practice of pilgrimage.[17] Over three hundred thousand registered pilgrims followed the Camino when our friends made the journey in 2018, although just over thirty thousand walked the entire route.[18]

From the reports I have heard and read, walking the Camino has been a transformational experience for so many. I have been so inspired by stories of returning pilgrims that I hope to make the journey someday. It would undoubtedly be a challenge of soul and body, but it is a challenge I am confident could be a great source of inspiration and encouragement. Yet there is one important difference between earthly pilgrimages like the Camino and the journey that Bunyan describes in *The Pilgrim's Progress*. When Christian and Hopeful finally reach heaven's gate, are transfigured into the likeness of Christ, and the bells of heaven ring with joy, it describes the time when we who walk by faith will reach our eternal home, where we will see with clarity and know in fullness even as we are known (1 Cor 13:12). Then the journey toward perfection will come to an end. As the apostle Paul says, at that point, the perfect has come, and the partial will pass away (1 Cor 13:10). When pilgrims from the Camino or any other earthly pilgrimage complete their journeys, they return home to continue struggling in this vale of tears. We are strangers and foreigners on earth, seeking our heavenly homeland. We desire a better country.

Let us not be ashamed that we are called and prepared by God to a final destination, a city whose builder and maker is God, a city not made with human hands (Heb 11:10–16). This is God's promise. This is our hope.

Yours in the journey,

Interpreter

Discussion Questions

Misery

1. *What strikes you as you look at the image of Christian and Evangelist?* Calm

2. *Reflect on the journey you have been on that got you here to this book seeking baptism. How has God moved in your life? Who has helped you get to this place?* He stands by like Evangelist pointing the way

3. *How can you see yourself in the biblical story as part of the people of Israel on a journey in the wilderness?* Struggle / challenge / hardship / fear / worry / faith

4. *Do you find it comforting to know that you are not alone in this journey and that Christians have been wrestling with these same principles for two thousand years?* Yes

5. *Why is it important for catechesis to occur not just in the church but also in the home?* Walk in the way

6. *How does the last verse of Bunyan's hymn describe what it means to be a Christian?*

Pilgrim's progress

7. What do you make of the fact that the wicket gate—that is, the door that leads to the church for Christian—is a small one? Is this an important detail?

[handwritten: one point of entry - Jesus]
[handwritten: We must]

PRINCIPLE 1 REPENTANCE

1. Looking at the body language and facial expression of the man with the open book, can you describe what he is feeling? Can you see yourself in the picture? How would you describe the way the burden is illustrated?

[handwritten: despair, desperation, weight of his condition, bearing his burden]
[handwritten: Causes one to stoop, to bend, it hurts]

2. The epigraph for this principle describes Christian leaving his home and traveling to the Celestial City. How does this explain the twofold action of repentance, of turning from my way to God's way? What would you have to leave behind to take your journey?

[handwritten: What I have is not what I seek or want... Turn toward the light - be drawn to Him.]

3. If you could tell God that you want to stop doing things your own way and to start following the way of Jesus, what would you say? Write it down and try saying it to God at the beginning and end of each day.

[handwritten: I want to see what You, God, will do and I do not want to "figure it out" on my own]

4. Explain what it means to "repent" in your own words. How is Interpreter's definition different from what you have previously understood?

[handwritten: Repent is to be horrified by one's sin & turning to God in submission for forgiveness]

5. Why is it important for the repentance to be the first step in the journey of Christian discipleship?

[handwritten: It is the letting go of "my way" It is yielding submitting acknowledging God]

At the cross, at the cross where I first saw the light, and the burden of my heart rolled away. It was there by faith I received my sight, and now I am happy all the day.

PRINCIPLE 2 FAITH

1. What is going on in the picture of Christian before the cross? *The burden of his sin "rolled away"*

2. Interpreter says, "Faith is neither an absolute certainty based on the facts nor a blind leap into the dark." Is this a scary idea or a <u>comforting one?</u> *(assurance, conviction, trust)*

3. Recite the Apostles' Creed twice each day for the next week at the beginning and end of each day. *Memorize*

4. Reflect on the words of Saint Anselm: "For I do not seek to understand in order that I may believe, but I believe in order to understand." How does faith fit into this model? *implies trust, not proof*

5. What is the significance of a profession of faith before baptism? *personal encounter + belief in Jesus comes before acceptance into the Body the Church*

6. Can you imagine living in such a way that your life is a living mystery that would not make sense if God did not exist? *"Temporary Home ... on a pilgrimage"*

PRINCIPLE 3 BAPTISM
If God doesn't exist then my life is w/o hope.

1. When you look at the image of Christian being helped out of the water, how does it make you think about your baptism? *My grandmother*

2. Why does Hebrews refer to "baptisms"? What are they? How are they united? *Water, Spirit, Suffering + Death*

3. How is baptism both a singular event and a lifelong journey? *initiation + growth under Lordship + unity w/ Christ*

4. Interpreter says that Christians have been baptizing one another since the first century in the name of the Father,

Son, and Holy Spirit. What does it mean that in baptism, we become members of the gathered community and the universal church? exactly that

5. *Try praying the Prayer of Saint Patrick every morning and night for one week.* p. 33   p. 37

I need God, Jesus + Holy Spirit

6. *What does it mean that we participate in the suffering, death, and resurrection of Christ in baptism?* p. 34 -35

7. *How is Hopeful's reply from the deep waters connected to our baptisms in Christ?* p. 38   the bottom

all is secure

PRINCIPLE 4 LAYING ON OF HANDS

God's messengers

1. *When you look at the image of Christian and the three messengers who greeted him, what do you see? Who are these visitors, and what do they represent? More importantly, who are these people in your life, and what are they saying and doing to you after baptism?* Mentors, encouragers

2. *How was the laying on of hands practiced in the Bible in ways that are not related to baptism? What is the significance of the laying on of hands?* Inheritance, missionaries receive the H.S.

3. *According to Acts 2:38, what is God's promise to us in baptism?*

4. *How is the laying on of hands related to the reception of the Holy Spirit?*

5. *What do prayer and the imposition of hands signify and ask God to do for the newly baptized believer?*

6. *How did the early church practice baptism, and how was the laying on of hands part of baptismal practice? How have churches today retrieved aspects of this practice?*

PRINCIPLE 5 RESURRECTION

1. *Look closely at the picture of Faithful rising up into heaven. What do you see? What might it mean?* Cross

2. *What is it about the resurrection of the dead that has troubled many Christians since the first Easter Sunday? Is this a principle that you wonder about as well?*
We cannot see it

3. *Why does Frederick Buechner suggest that doubt can be a positive experience for some Christians?*
leads to seeking + learning

4. *How does the church give us language that enables us to see the promise of resurrection?* Faith comes from what is heard

5. *Paul declares in 2 Corinthians 5:17 that in Christ, we see a completely new creation. How is the resurrection the turning point in this history? What does his resurrection assure us about the future?* Different life - complete union w/ God

6. *How does baptism dramatically enact and signify the promise of resurrection?* We are cleansed, buried + raised to walk in new life

PRINCIPLE 6 ETERNAL JUDGMENT

1. *Look at the picture of the man who dreamed of judgment, and read his words in the quote beneath the image. Have you ever awoken from a dream where you were afraid? Are you concerned about the future?*

2. When you have thought before about eternal judgment, did you consider it to be a terrifying and harsh process? Does Interpreter's explanation make you think differently about it?

3. How does Interpreter shift the understanding of final judgment from strictly a future occurrence to an event that should shape our lives now?

4. Interpreter says, "Things eternal come last, but things are eternal because they last." How does this statement help us understand the parable of the wise and foolish bridesmaids in Matthew 25:1–13?

5. What virtue are we called to cultivate in our lives now that will live on eternally, and why does it last forever?

6. What is God's final word, and how is it spoken in Jesus? How does this change your understanding of the eternal judgment?

CONCLUSION: GOING ON TOWARD PERFECTION

1. What do you see in the picture of Christian and Hopeful as they near the Celestial City? How do you see this fitting into your faith journey?

2. Do you find yourself "stuck" in any areas of your faith journey from time to time? Does Interpreter's letter help you get moving again?

3. In what ways can "pilgrimage" be both a geographical journey and a theological endeavor? How are they different?

4. *The Interpreter gives several definitions of what it means to go on toward perfection. In your own words, what does it mean to seek perfection?*

5. *What did Egeria learn from Cyril and the church in Jerusalem, and how do the mysteries nurture and sustain us to live by faith in our pilgrimages to the Holy City?*

6. *As you move toward perfection, who is someone you could walk the path with to push you and guide you?*

Notes

PREFACE

1   John D. Lockhart, "Laying Foundations of Faith," *Christian Reflection* 23 (2007): 66–72, accessed April 7, 2020, https://tinyurl.com/y3wtoeph.

2   Tertullian, "Apology," trans. S. Thelwall, in *The Ante-Nicene Fathers*, ed. A. Cleveland Coxe (Grand Rapids: Eerdmans, 1978), 3:32.

3   Benedict XVI, "Homily of First Vespers on the Solemnity of the Holy Apostles Peter and Paul," Vatican Publishing House, accessed April 9, 2020, https://tinyurl.com/68xz63o.

4   While the possibility that infant baptism may have been practiced in the apostolic age cannot be excluded, as Everett Ferguson suggests, the earliest uncontested reference to infant baptism is in Irenaeus, *Against Heresies* 2.22.4, in Ferguson, *Baptism in the Early Church* (Grand Rapids: Eerdmans, 2009), 308.

5   *Baptism, Eucharist and Ministry* IV.A.11, Faith and Order Paper No. 111 (Geneva, Switzerland: World Council of Churches, 1982), 4.

Introduction: Basic Teaching

1   John Bunyan, *The Pilgrim's Progress*, retold and shortened for modern readers by Mary Godolphin (Philadelphia: J. B. Lippincott, 1884), 3.

2   Tertullian, "On Baptism," 18, trans. S. Thelwall, in *The Ante-Nicene Fathers*, ed. A. Cleveland Coxe (Grand Rapids: Eerdmans, 1978), 3:678.

3   James Wm. McClendon Jr., "Baptism as a Performative Sign," *Theology Today* 23, no. 3 (October 1966): 403–416, esp. 407 and 413.

4   C. S. Lewis, *Mere Christianity* (New York: Macmillan, 1952).

5   James A. Kleist, trans., *Didache*, 1.2, in *Ancient Christian Writers* (New York: Newman Press, 1948), 6:15.

6   Isaac Watts, "Broad Is the Road That Leads to Death," in *Hymns and Spiritual Songs: In Three Books* (London: J. Humfreys for John Lawrence, 1709), book 2, no. 158.

7   Martin Luther, *Small Catechism* (Philadelphia: General Council Publication Board, 1874).

8   Thomas Grantham, *St. Paul's Catechism*, 2nd ed. (London: J. Darby, 1693). It is called *St. Paul's Catechism* because it was traditionally thought that the Epistle to the Hebrews was written by the apostle Paul. The consensus among modern biblical scholars is that the author of Hebrews is unknown.

9   Catholic Church, *Rite of Christian Initiation of Adults*, study ed. (Chicago: Archdiocese of Chicago, Liturgy Training, 1988); and Gregory Dix and Henry Chadwick, eds., *The Treatise on the Apostolic Tradition of St. Hippolytus of Rome* (London: Alban Press, 1992).

10 Tommy Bratton, Casey Callahan, Mack Dennis, and Amy Stertz, *Via Karis* (Asheville, NC: First Baptist Church, 2018).

11 Augustine, *City of God*, 15.20, trans. Henry Bettenson (New York: Penguin, 1984), 630.

12 John Bunyan, *The Pilgrim's Progress*, ed. N. H. Keeble (New York: Oxford University Press, 1984), 247.

PRINCIPLE 1 REPENTANCE

1 John Bunyan, *The Pilgrim's Progress*, retold and shortened for modern readers by Mary Godolphin (Philadelphia: J. B. Lippincott, 1884), 1.

2 Mark Twain, *The Adventures of Huckleberry Finn* (New York: Puffin Books, 1994), 14.

3 James A. Kleist, trans., *Didache*, 8.3, in *Ancient Christian Writers* (New York: Newman Press, 1948), 6:19.

4 Kara K. Root, "The 20-Second Gift of Washing Your Hands," *Faith & Leadership*, March 12, 2020, accessed March 18, 2020, https://tinyurl.com/yddjrewa.

5 Martin Luther, "The Ninety-Five Theses," thesis 1, trans. C. M. Jacobs, in *Luther's Works*, vol. 31, ed. Helmut T. Lehmann (Philadelphia: Muhlenberg, 1957), 25.

6 "Standing in the Need of Prayer," traditional.

7 Michael Sattler, *Schleitheim Articles*, article 1, trans. and ed. John H. Yoder (Scottdale, PA: Herald, 1973), 36.

8 Edward Barber, *A Small Treatise of Baptisme or Dipping* (London, 1641), 4.

9 Tertullian, "On Baptism," 18, trans. S. Thelwall, in *The Ante-Nicene Fathers*, ed. A. Cleveland Coxe (Grand Rapids: Eerdmans, 1978), 3:678.

10 Francis Spufford, *Unapologetic: Why, Despite Everything, Christianity Can Still Make Surprising Emotional Sense* (New York: Harper, 2013), 27.

11 William Faulkner, *Requiem for a Nun* (Bungay, Suffolk: Penguin, 1953), 233; cited by Shirley C. Guthrie, *Christian Doctrine*, rev. ed. (Louisville: Westminster / John Knox, 1994), 221.

12 The phrase "Let go and let God" is a slogan that summarizes steps 1–3 of "The Twelve Steps" of A. A., in Bill W., *Alcoholics Anonymous*, 3rd ed. (New York: Alcoholic Anonymous World Services, 1976), 59. This is also known as "The Big Book." These three steps are sometimes abbreviated: (1) I can't, (2) God can, and (3) I think I'll let God.

13 C. S. Lewis, *The Screwtape Letters* (New York: Macmillan, 1961), 3.

14 Hendrik Berkhof, *Christ and the Powers*, trans. and ed. John H. Yoder (Scottdale, PA: Herald, 1962), 13–17; Walter Wink, *Engaging the Powers: Discernment and Resistance in a World of Domination* (Minneapolis: Fortress Press, 1992), 1–9.

15 James R. Brockman, *Oscar Romero: Bishop and Martyr* (Maryknoll, NY: Orbis, 1982).

16 Hippolytus, "The Apostolic Tradition," 21.9–10, in *The Treatise on the Apostolic Tradition of St. Hippolytus of Rome*, ed. Gregory Dix and Henry Chadwick (London: Alban Press, 1992), 34–35.

17 Daniel Defoe, *Robinson Crusoe*, ed. Michael Shinagel (New York: W. W. Norton, 1994), 13.

18 "Catechism: The Six Principles," principle 1, page xiii.

19 Helen Bacovcin, trans., *The Way of a Pilgrim and the Pilgrim Continues His Way* (New York: Image/Doubleday, 1992).

20 Abba Lucius, s.v. "Lambda/Lucius," in *The Sayings of the Desert Fathers*, trans. Benedicta Ward (Kalamazoo, MI: Cistercian, 1984), 120–121.

21 Bunyan, *Pilgrim's Progress*, 1.

22 John Bunyan, *The Pilgrim's Progress*, ed. N. H. Keeble (New York: Oxford University Press, 1984), 46.

PRINCIPLE 2 FAITH

1 John Bunyan, *The Pilgrim's Progress*, retold and shortened for modern readers by Mary Godolphin (Philadelphia: J. B. Lippincott, 1884), 22.

2 Charles Taylor, *A Secular Age* (Cambridge: Belknap Press, 2007), 1–3; and James K. A. Smith, *How (Not) to Be Secular: Reading Charles Taylor* (Grand Rapids: Eerdmans, 2014). The secular age is not characterized by unbelief. Rather, it is a world where a shared belief structure is no longer the default position of the whole society. All beliefs are contested and contestable.

3 Clarence Jordan, *The Substance of Faith* (Eugene, OR: Cascade, 2005), 43.

4 Lewis Carroll, *Alice's Adventures in Wonderland and Through the Looking-Glass* (New York: Barnes & Noble Classics, 2004), 207.

5   Anselm, "Proslogion," 1, lines 134–142, 154–157, in *The Prayers and Meditations of Saint Anselm*, trans. Benedicta Ward (New York: Penguin, 1973), 243–244.

6   Jaroslav Pelikan, *Credo: Historical and Theological Guide to Creeds and Confessions of Faith in the Christian Tradition* (New Haven: Yale University Press, 2003), 1–5.

7   English Language Liturgical Commission (ELLC), trans., "The Apostles' Creed," in *Praying Together* (Nashville: Abingdon, 1988), 22, https://tinyurl.com/y4n8tyye. See Ben Myers, *The Apostles' Creed: A Guide to the Ancient Catechism* (Bellingham, WA: Lexham Press, 2018).

8   Gregory of Nazianzus, "Oration," 38.7, trans. Charles Gordon Browne and James Edward Swallow, in *The Nicene and Post-Nicene Fathers, Second Series*, ed. Philip Schaff and Henry Wace (Grand Rapids: Eerdmans, 1978), 7:347.

9   Augustine, "On the Trinity," 15.2.2, trans. Arthur West Haddan and William G. T. Shedd, in *The Nicene and Post-Nicene Fathers*, ed. Philip Schaff (Grand Rapids: Eerdmans, 1978), 3:200.

10 Kathleen Norris, *Amazing Grace* (New York: Riverhead Books, 1998), 64–65.

11 My friend Kyle Childress, who told this story, was at that protest in Atlanta, Georgia, in 1985 when C. T. Vivian prayed.

12 John Bunyan, *The Pilgrim's Progress*, ed. N. H. Keeble (New York: Oxford University Press, 1984), 31.

13 Dorothy Day, *On Pilgrimage* (Grand Rapids: Eerdmans, 1999), 85.

14 Robert Coles, *Dorothy Day: A Radical Devotion* (Reading, MA: Addison-Wesley, 1987), 160.

PRINCIPLE 3 BAPTISM

1   John Bunyan, *The Pilgrim's Progress*, retold and shortened for modern readers by Mary Godolphin (Philadelphia: J. B. Lippincott, 1884), 8.

2   Paul S. Fiddes, "Baptism and the Process of Christian Initiation," *Ecumenical Review* 54, no. 1 (2002): 48–65. The emphasis of placing baptism within the whole process of Christian

initiation is one of the contributions of the ecumenical retrieval of catechesis in the early church. As James Wm. McClendon Jr. reported, Baptist theologians in the second half of the twentieth century have likewise insisted "that baptism is initiation into the full life of the church—and thus is related to the word, to the Lord's Supper, and to the shared life of worship and service in the church." "Baptism as a Performative Sign," *Theology Today* 23, no. 3 (October 1966): 406.

3 *Baptism, Eucharist and Ministry*, IV.B.14, Faith and Order Paper No. 111 (Geneva, Switzerland: World Council of Churches, 1982), 4–6.

4 "Catechism: The Six Principles," principle 3, page xiv.

5 James A. Kleist, trans., *Didache*, 7.1–3, in *Ancient Christian Writers* (New York: Newman Press, 1948), 6:19.

6 Cecil Frances Alexander, "St. Patrick's Breastplate," in *Poems*, ed. William Alexander (London: Macmillan, 1897), 59.

7 Edward Barber, *A Small Treatise of Baptisme or Dipping* (London, 1641), 2.

8 Tertullian, "On Baptism," 18, trans. S. Thelwall, in *The Ante-Nicene Fathers*, ed. A. Cleveland Coxe (Grand Rapids: Eerdmans, 1978), 3:678.

9 Leonard Busher, "Religion's Peace; Or, a Plea for Liberty of Conscience," in *Tracts on Liberty of Conscience and Persecution*, ed. Edward Bean Underhill (London: Hanserd Knollys Society, 1846), 59.

10 Martin Luther, "The Babylonian Captivity of the Church," trans. A. T. W. Steinhäuser and revised by Frederick C. Ahrens and Abdel Ross Wentz, in *Luther's Works*, vol. 36, ed. Abdel Ross Wentz (Philadelphia: Fortress Press, 1958), 112–113.

11 William Carey, *An Enquiry into the Obligations of Christians to Use Means for the Conversion of the Heathens* (1792; repr., London: Carey Kingsgate Press, 1961), 7–13.

12 Alexander, "St. Patrick's Breastplate," 61.

13 John Bunyan, *The Pilgrim's Progress*, ed. N. H. Keeble (New York: Oxford University Press, 1984), 12–13.

14 Bunyan, 128.

15 George Keith, "How Firm a Foundation," in *A Selection of Hymns from the Best Authors: Intended to Be an Appendix to Dr. Watts's*

Psalms and Hymns, by John Rippon (London: Thomas Wilkins, 1787), 128.

16 Robert Browning, "Pippa Passes," act 1, in *The Poetical Works of Robert Browning*, ed. Augustine Birrell (London: Smith, Elder, 1897), 1:202.

PRINCIPLE 4 LAYING ON OF HANDS

1 John Bunyan, *The Pilgrim's Progress*, ed. N. H. Keeble (New York: Oxford University Press, 1984), 31–32.

2 David P. Wright, "The Gesture of Hand Placement in the Hebrew Bible and in Hittite Literature," *Journal of the American Oriental Society* 106, no. 3 (July–September 1986): 433–446.

3 Hippolytus, "The Apostolic Tradition," 19.1, in *The Treatise on the Apostolic Tradition of St. Hippolytus of Rome*, ed. Gregory Dix and Henry Chadwick (London: Alban Press, 1992), 30.

4 Tertullian, "On Baptism," 8–9, trans. S. Thelwall, in *The Ante-Nicene Fathers*, ed. A. Cleveland Coxe (Grand Rapids: Eerdmans, 1978), 3:672–673.

5 George Beasley-Murray, *Baptism in the New Testament* (Grand Rapids: Eerdmans, 1962), 121–122.

6 Catholic Church, *Rite of Christian Initiation of Adults*, study ed. (Chicago: Archdiocese of Chicago, Liturgy Training, 1988), 115–122, 334.

7 Evangelical Lutheran Church of America, *Evangelical Lutheran Worship* (Minneapolis: Augsburg, 2006), 234–237.

8 Thomas Grantham, *St. Paul's Catechism*, 2nd ed. (London: J. Darby, 1693), 32–35; and Hercules Collins, *An Orthodox Catechism* (London, 1680), 36–38.

9 John Griffith, "The Six Principles of Christian Religion," in *Two Discourses*, ed. Joseph Jenkins (London: R. Tookey, 1707), 112.

10 "The Philadelphia Confession," 31, in *Baptist Confessions of Faith*, ed. William L. Lumpkin, rev. ed. (Valley Forge, PA: Judson, 1969), 351.

11 Morgan Edwards, *The Customs of Primitive Churches* (Philadelphia, 1774), 82–83.

12 Christopher Ellis and Myra Blyth, *Gathering for Worship* (Norwich, England: Canterbury, 2005), 64–93.

13 Bunyan, *Pilgrim's Progress*, 31–32.

PRINCIPLE 5 RESURRECTION

1 John Bunyan, *The Pilgrim's Progress*, ed. N. H. Keeble (New York: Oxford University Press, 1984), 80.

2 Jimmy Carter, *Living Faith* (New York: Random House, 1996), 17.

3 Frederick Buechner, *Wishful Thinking: A Theological ABC* (San Francisco: Harper, 1970), 20.

4 Stanley Hauerwas, *The Work of Theology* (Grand Rapids: Eerdmans, 2015), 26–29.

5 English Language Liturgical Commission (ELLC), trans., "The Apostles' Creed," in *Praying Together* (Nashville: Abingdon, 1988), https://tinyurl.com/y4n8tyye.

6 Aidan Kavanaugh, "A Rite of Passage," in *Primary Source Readings in Catholic History*, ed. Robert Feduccia Jr. (Winona, MN: St. Mary's Press, 2005), 11–16.

7 Rowan Williams, *Resurrection* (New York: Pilgrim Press, 1984), 63.

8 Tertullian, "On the Resurrection of the Flesh," 8, trans. Peter Holmes, in *The Ante-Nicene Fathers*, ed. A. Cleveland Coxe (Grand Rapids: Eerdmans, 1978), 3:551.

9 Tertullian, "Resurrection of the Flesh," 63, in *Ante-Nicene Fathers*, 3:593.

10 Martin Luther, "Of Baptism," no. 292, in *The Table Talk of Martin Luther*, ed. Thomas S. Kepler (Mineola, NY: Dover, 2005), 120.

11 "Catechism: The Six Principles," principle 5, page xiv.

12 Dietrich Bonhoeffer, letter to Eberhard Bethge, December 5, 1943, in *Letters and Papers from Prison*, ed. Eberhard Bethge and trans. R. H. Fuller (New York: Macmillan, 1972), 157.

13 Bonhoeffer, *The Cost of Discipleship*, trans. R. H. Fuller (New York: Macmillan, 1966), 99.

14 Bunyan, *Pilgrim's Progress*, 80.

15 George Keith, "How Firm a Foundation," in *A Selection of Hymns from the Best Authors: Intended to Be an Appendix to Dr. Watts's*

Psalms and Hymns, by John Rippon (London: Thomas Wilkins, 1787), 128.

16 Thieleman J. van Braght, *The Bloody Theater or Martyrs Mirror of the Defenseless Christians, Who Baptized Only upon Confession of Faith, and Who Suffered and Died for the Testimony of Jesus, Their Savior, from the Time of Christ to the Year A.D. 1660*, trans. Joseph F. Sohm (Scottdale, PA: Herald, 1987), 659–660.

PRINCIPLE 6 ETERNAL JUDGMENT

1 John Bunyan, *The Pilgrim's Progress*, ed. N. H. Keeble (New York: Oxford University Press, 1984), 30.

2 Henry Jessey, *A Catechism for Babies, or Little Ones*, "The First Catechism," 4, in *Baptist Confessions, Covenants, and Catechisms*, ed. Timothy George and Denise George (Nashville: Broadman, 1996), 236.

3 Bunyan, *Pilgrim's Progress*, 29–31.

4 Jonathan Edwards, "Sinners in the Hands of an Angry God," in *The Works of Jonathan Edwards*, vol. 22, *Sermons and Discourses (1739–1742)*, ed. Harry S. Stout and Nathan O. Hatch (New Haven: Yale University Press, 2003), 410.

5 Edwards, 412.

6 James Weldon Johnson, *God's Trombones* (New York: Penguin, 1969), 11.

7 Frederick Buechner, *Telling the Truth* (New York: Harper, 1977), 7.

8 Johnson, *God's Trombones*, 53, 59.

9 H. Richard Niebuhr, *The Kingdom of God in America* (New York: Harper, 1937; repr., Middletown, CT: Wesleyan University Press, 1988), 193. Page references are to the 1988 edition.

10 James Wm. McClendon Jr., *Doctrine: Systematic Theology* (Waco, TX: Baylor University Press, 2012), 2:75–77.

11 McClendon, 79.

12 Henry Drummond, *The Greatest Thing in the World* (London: Hodder and Stoughton, 1891), 24.

13 Drummond, 58–59.

14 Bunyan, *Pilgrim's Progress*, 8–9.

15 Karl Barth, *Church Dogmatics*, trans. G. W. Bromiley (Edinburgh, Scotland: T. & T. Clark, 1956), 4/1:211–283.

16 "Boundless Love," track 8 on John Prine, *The Tree of Forgiveness*, Oh Boy, 2018.

17 Pope Francis, *The Name of God Is Mercy: A Conversation with Andrea Tornielli*, trans. Oonagh Stransky (New York: Random House, 2016), 85.

CONCLUSION: GOING ON TOWARD PERFECTION

1 John Bunyan, *The Pilgrim's Progress*, ed. N. H. Keeble (New York: Oxford University Press, 1984), 132–133. I have slightly paraphrased and modernized Bunyan's language.

2 Christian Smith with Melinda Lundquist Denton, *Soul Searching: The Religious and Spiritual Lives of American Teenagers* (New York: Oxford University Press, 2005), 118–171.

3 John Wesley, "A Plain Account of Christian Perfection," in *Doctrinal and Controversial Treatises II*, vol. 13 of *The Works of John Wesley*, ed. Paul Wesley Chilcote and Kenneth J. Collins (Nashville: Abingdon, 2013), 132–191.

4 United Methodist Church, *The Book of Discipline of the United Methodist Church* (Nashville: United Methodist Publishing House, 2016), ¶336/270.

5 Emil Brunner, *The Divine Human Encounter*, trans. Amandus W. Loos (Philadelphia: Westminster, 1943), 181.

6 Alasdair MacIntyre, *After Virtue: A Study in Moral Theory* (Notre Dame: University of Notre Dame Press, 1981), 49–59.

7 Presbyterian Committee of Publication, *The Westminster Shorter Catechism*, 1 (Richmond, VA: Presbyterian Committee of Publication, 1862).

8 Arthur Dent, *The Plain Man's Pathway to Heaven*, 15th ed. (London, 1601; Belfast: North of Ireland Book and Tract Depository, 1859).

9 *The Geneva Bible*, 1560 ed. (repr., Madison: University of Wisconsin Press, 1969).

10 Cited by N. H. Keeble, "To Be a Pilgrim," in *Pilgrimage: The English Experience from Becket to Bunyan*, ed. Colin Morris

and Peter Roberts (Cambridge: Cambridge University Press, 2002), 247.

11 Augustine, "Sermons on the Psalms," 149.3, trans. J. E. Tweed, in *The Nicene and Post-Nicene Fathers*, ed. A. Cleveland Coxe and Philip Schaff (Grand Rapids: Eerdmans, 1979), 8:678.

12 John Wilkinson, ed. and trans., *Egeria's Travels to the Holy Land*, 45–47, revised ed. (Jerusalem: Ariel, 1981), 143–146.

13 Cyril of Jerusalem, "Catechetical Lectures," 19–23, trans. Edwin Hamilton Gifford, in *The Nicene and Post-Nicene Fathers*, ed. Philip Schaff (Grand Rapids: Eerdmans, 1978), 7:144–157.

14 Augustine, "Sermon 272," in *Ad Infantes, de Sacramento, in Patrologia Latina*, ed. J. P. Migne (Paris: Migne, 1865), 38:1246–1248.

15 "The Orthodox Creed," 19, in *Baptist Confessions of Faith*, ed. William L. Lumpkin, rev. ed. (Valley Forge, PA: Judson, 1969), 311–312.

16 Edward Winslow, *Hypocrisie Unmasked* (London: Rich. Cotes, 1646; repr., New York: Burt Franklin, 1968), 97–98 (page references are to the 1968 edition); and William Bradford, *History "Of Plimouth Plantation"* (Boston: Wright and Potter, 1899), 71–83.

17 Rubén C. Lois González, "The Camino De Santiago and Its Contemporary Renewal: Pilgrims, Tourists, and Territorial Identities," *Culture and Religion* 14, no. 1 (2013): 8–22.

18 Laurie A. Ferris, "30 Years of Pilgrim Statistics," *Camino Provides*, January 31, 2017, https://tinyurl.com/ybawlatf. For 2018 statistics, see Oficina del Peregrino, "Informe Estadístico Año 2018," Oficina del Peregrino, accessed April 7, 2020, https://tinyurl.com/yd9jdtsh.

Bibliography

FURTHER READINGS

Baker, J. Robert, Larry J. Nyberg, and Victoria M. Tufano, eds. *A Baptism Sourcebook*. Chicago: Archdiocese of Chicago, Liturgy Training, 1993.

Benedict, Daniel T., Jr. *Come to the Waters: Baptism and Our Ministry of Welcoming Seekers and Making Disciples*. Nashville: Discipleship Resources, 1997.

Blyth, Myra, and Andy Goodliff, eds. *Gathering Disciples*. Eugene, OR: Pickwick, 2017.

Edie, Fred P. *Book, Bath, Table, and Time: Christian Worship as Source and Response for Youth Ministry*. Cleveland, OH: Pilgrim Press, 2007.

Episcopal Church Center, Office of Evangelism Ministries, *The Catechumenal Process: Adult Initiation and Formation for Christian Life and Ministry*. New York: Church Hymnal Corporation, 1990.

Fiddes, Paul S., ed. *Reflections on the Waters: Understanding God and the World through the Baptism of Believers*. Macon, GA: Smyth and Helwys, 1996.

Hansen, Collin, ed. *The New City Catechism Devotional: God's Truth for Our Hearts and Minds*. Wheaton, IL: Crossway, 2017.

Harmless, William. *Augustine and the Catechumenate*. Collegeville, MN: Liturgical, 2014.

Hauerwas, Stanley. *The Character of Virtue*. Grand Rapids: Eerdmans, 2018.

Hollon, Bryan C. "Catechesis and Christian Discipleship." *Knowing and Doing*, Spring 2019, 1–23. Accessed April 7, 2020. https://tinyurl.com/yaka7c8t.

Johnson, Keith L. *Theology as Discipleship*. Downers Grove, IL: Intervarsity, 2015.

Kreider, Alan. "Catechesis and Baptism." In *The Patient Ferment of the Early Church*, 133–184. Grand Rapids: Baker Academic, 2016.

Kruschwitz, Robert B., ed. "Catechism." Center for Christian Ethics at Baylor University. *Christian Reflection* 23 (2007). Accessed April 7, 2020. https://tinyurl.com/y3wtoeph.

Merriman, Michael W., ed. *The Baptismal Mystery and the Catechumenate*. New York: Church Publishing, 1990.

Morris, Thomas H. *The RCIA: Transforming the Church*. New York: Paulist, 1997.

Nelson, Paul, et al. *Welcome to Christ: A Lutheran Introduction to the Catechumenate*. Minneapolis: Augsburg Fortress Press, 1997.

Osmer, Richard, and Katherine M. Douglas, eds. *Cultivating Teen Faith: Insights from the Confirmation Project*. Grand Rapids: Eerdmans, 2018.

Packer, J. I., and Gary A. Parrett. *Grounded in the Gospel: Building Believers the Old-Fashioned Way*. Grand Rapids: Baker, 2010.

Peifer, Jane Hoober, and John Stahl-Wert. *Welcoming New Christians: A Guide for the Christian Initiation of Adults*. Newton, KS: Faith and Life, 1995.

Wilde, James A., ed. *Before and after Baptism: The Work of Teachers and Catechists*. Chicago: Archdiocese of Chicago, Liturgy Training, 1988.

———. *Commentaries on the Rite of Christian Initiation of Adults*. Chicago: Archdiocese of Chicago, Liturgy Training, 1988.

Wilken, Robert Louis. "The Church's Way of Speaking." *First Things* 155 (August–September 2005): 27–31.

Willimon, William H. *Remember Who You Are: Baptism as a Model for the Christian Life*. Nashville: Upper Room, 1980.

Winner, Lauren. *The Dangers of Christian Practice: On Wayward Gifts, Characteristic Damage, and Sin*. New Haven: Yale University Press, 2018.

Wood, Susan K. "Is Baptism Complete or Part of a Larger Christian Initiation?" *Seminary Ridge Review* 17, no. 2 (Spring 2015): 35–47.

SOURCES CITED

Alexander, Cecil Frances. "St. Patrick's Breastplate." In *Poems*, edited by William Alexander, 59–62. London: Macmillan, 1897.

Anselm. *The Prayers and Meditations of Saint Anselm*. Translated by Benedicta Ward. New York: Penguin, 1973.

Augustine. *City of God*. Translated by Henry Bettenson. New York: Penguin, 1984.

———. "On the Trinity." Translated by Arthur West Haddan and William G. T. Shedd. In *The Nicene and Post-Nicene Fathers*, edited by Philip Schaff, 1–228. Vol. 3. Grand Rapids: Eerdmans, 1978.

———. "Sermons on the Psalms." Translated by J. E. Tweed. In *The Nicene and Post-Nicene Fathers*, edited by A. Cleveland Coxe and Philip Schaff. Vol. 8. Grand Rapids: Eerdmans, 1979.

———. "Sermon 272." In *Ad Infantes, de Sacramento. Patrologia Latina*, edited by J. P. Migne, 1246–1248. Vol. 38. Paris: Migne, 1865.

Bacovcin, Helen, trans. *The Way of a Pilgrim and The Pilgrim Continues His Way*. New York: Image/Doubleday, 1992.

Baptism, Eucharist, and Ministry. Faith and Order Paper No. 111, "The Lima Text." Geneva, Switzerland: World Council of Churches, 1982.

Barber, Edward. *A Small Treatise of Baptisme or Dipping*. London, 1641.

Barth, Karl. *Church Dogmatics*. Translated by G. W. Bromiley. Vol. 4/1. Edinburgh, Scotland: T. & T. Clark, 1956.

Beasley-Murray, George. *Baptism in the New Testament*. Grand Rapids: Eerdmans, 1962.

Benedict XVI. "Homily of First Vespers on the Solemnity of the Holy Apostles Peter and Paul." Vatican Publishing House. Accessed April 9, 2020. https://tinyurl.com/68xz63o.

Berkhof, Hendrik. *Christ and the Powers*. Translated by John H. Yoder. Scottdale, PA: Herald, 1962.

Bonhoeffer, Dietrich. *The Cost of Discipleship*. Translated by R. H. Fuller. New York: Macmillan, 1966.

————. *Letters and Papers from Prison*. Edited by Eberhard Bethge. Translated by R. H. Fuller. New York: Macmillan, 1972.

Bradford, William. *History "Of Plimoth Plantation."* Boston: Wright and Potter, 1899.

Braght, Thieleman J. van. *The Bloody Theater or Martyrs Mirror of the Defenseless Christians, Who Baptized Only upon Confession of Faith, and Who Suffered and Died for the Testimony of Jesus, Their Savior, from the Time of Christ to the Year A.D. 1660*. Translated Joseph F. Sohm. Scottdale, PA: Herald, 1987.

Bratton, Tommy, Casey Callahan, Mack Dennis, and Amy Stertz. *Via Karis*. Asheville, NC: First Baptist Church, 2018.

Brockman, James R. *Oscar Romero: Bishop and Martyr*. Maryknoll, NY: Orbis, 1982.

Browning, Robert. *The Poetical Works of Robert Browning*. 2 vols. London: Smith, Elder, 1897.

Brunner, Emil. *The Divine Human Encounter*. Translated by Amandus W. Loos. Philadelphia: Westminster, 1943.

Buechner, Frederick. *Telling the Truth*. New York: Harper, 1977.

————. *Wishful Thinking: A Theological ABC*. San Francisco: Harper, 1970.

Bunyan, John. *The Pilgrim's Progress*. Edited by N. H. Keeble. New York: Oxford University Press, 1984.

————. *The Pilgrim's Progress*. Modernized by Mary Godolphin. Philadelphia: J. B. Lippincott, 1939.

Busher, Leonard. "Religion's Peace; Or, a Plea for Liberty of Conscience." In *Tracts on Liberty of Conscience and Persecution*, edited by Edward Bean Underhill, 1–81. London: Hanserd Knollys Society, 1846.

Carey, William. *An Enquiry into the Obligations of Christians to Use Means for the Conversion of the Heathens*. London: Carey Kingsgate Press, 1961. First published in 1792.

Carroll, Lewis. *Alice's Adventures in Wonderland and Through the Looking-Glass*. New York: Barnes & Noble Classics, 2004.

Carter, Jimmy. *Living Faith*. New York: Random House, 1996.

Catholic Church. *Rite of Christian Initiation of Adults*. Study ed. Chicago: Archdiocese of Chicago, Liturgy Training, 1988.

Coles, Robert. *Dorothy Day: A Radical Devotion*. Reading, MA: Addison-Wesley, 1987.

Collins, Hercules. *An Orthodox Catechism*. London, 1680.

Cyril of Jerusalem. "Catechetical Lectures." Translated by Edward Hamilton Gifford. In *The Nicene and Post-Nicene Fathers*, edited by Philip Schaff and Henry Wace, 1–183. Vol. 7. Grand Rapids: Eerdmans, 1978.

Day, Dorothy. *On Pilgrimage*. Grand Rapids: Eerdmans, 1999.

Defoe, Daniel. *Robinson Crusoe*. Edited by Michael Shinagel. New York: W. W. Norton, 1994.

Dent, Arthur. *The Plain Man's Pathway to Heaven*. 15th ed. Belfast: North of Ireland Book and Tract Depository, 1859. First published in 1601 (London).

Drummond, Henry. *The Greatest Thing in the World*. London: Hodder and Stoughton, 1891.

Edwards, Jonathan. "Sinners in the Hands of an Angry God." In *Sermons and Discourses (1739–1742)*, edited by Harry S. Stout and Nathan O. Hatch with Kyle P. Farley, 404–418. Vol. 22 of *The Works of Jonathan Edwards*. New Haven: Yale University Press, 2003.

Edwards, Morgan. *The Customs of Primitive Churches*. Philadelphia, 1774.

Ellis, Christopher, and Myra Blyth. *Gathering for Worship: Patterns and Prayers for the Community of Disciples*. Norwich, England: Canterbury, 2005.

English Language Liturgical Commission (ELLC). *Praying Together*. Nashville: Abingdon, 1988.

Evangelical Lutheran Church of America. *Evangelical Lutheran Worship*. Minneapolis: Augsburg, 2006.

Faulkner, William. *Requiem for a Nun*. Bungay, Suffolk: Penguin, 1953.

Ferris, Laurie A. "30 Years of Pilgrim Statistics." *Camino Provides*, January 31, 2017. https://tinyurl.com/ybawlatf.

Fiddes, Paul S. "Baptism and the Process of Christian Initiation." *Ecumenical Review* 54, no. 1 (2002): 48–65.

Francis, Pope. *The Name of God Is Mercy: A Conversation with Andrea Tornielli*. Translated by Oonagh Stransky. New York: Random House, 2016.

The Geneva Bible. 1560 ed. Reprint, Madison: University of Wisconsin Press, 1969.

George, Timothy, and Denise George, eds. *Baptist Confessions, Covenants, and Catechisms*. Nashville: Broadman, 1996.

González, Rubén C. Lois. "The Camino de Santiago and Its Contemporary Renewal: Pilgrims, Tourists, and Territorial Identities." *Culture and Religion* 14, no. 1 (2013): 8–22.

Grantham, Thomas. *St. Paul's Catechism*. 2nd ed. London: J. Darby, 1693.

Gregory of Nazianzus. "Oration 38 'On the Theophany, or Birthday of Christ.'" Translated by Charles Gordon Browne and James Edward Swallow. In *The Nicene and Post-Nicene Fathers, Second Series*, edited by Philip Schaff and Henry Wace, 345–351. Vol. 7. Grand Rapids: Eerdmans, 1978.

Griffith, John. "The Six Principles of Christian Religion." In *Two Discourses*, edited by Joseph Jenkins, 1–208. London: R. Tookey, 1707.

Guthrie, Shirley C. *Christian Doctrine*. Rev. ed. Louisville: Westminster / John Knox, 1994.

Hauerwas, Stanley. *The Work of Theology*. Grand Rapids: Eerdmans, 2015.

Hippolytus. *The Treatise on the Apostolic Tradition of St. Hippolytus of Rome*. Edited by Gregory Dix and Henry Chadwick. London: Alban Press, 1992.

Irenaeus. *Against Heresies* 2.22.4. In *Baptism in the Early Church*. Grand Rapids: Eerdmans, 2009.

Johnson, James Weldon. *God's Trombones*. New York: Penguin, 1969.

Jordan, Clarence. *The Substance of Faith*. Eugene, OR: Cascade, 2005.

Kavanaugh, Aidan. "A Rite of Passage." In *Primary Source Readings in Catholic History*, edited by Robert Feduccia Jr., 11–16. Winona, MN: St. Mary's Press, 2005.

Kleist, James A., trans. *Didache*. In *Ancient Christian Writers*, 1–25. Vol. 6. New York: Newman Press, 1948.

Lewis, C. S. *Mere Christianity*. New York: Macmillan, 1952.

———. *The Screwtape Letters*. New York: Macmillan, 1961.

Lockhart, John D. "Laying Foundations of Faith." *Christian Reflection* 23 (2007): 66–72. https://tinyurl.com/y3wtoeph.

Lumpkin, William L. *Baptist Confessions of Faith*. Rev. ed. Valley Forge, PA: Judson, 1969.

Luther, Martin. "The Babylonian Captivity of the Church." Translated by A. T. W. Steinhäuser and revised by Frederick C. Ahrens and Abdel Ross Wentz. In *Luther's Works*, edited by Abdel Ross Wentz, 11–126. Vol. 36. Philadelphia: Fortress Press, 1958.

———. "The Ninety-Five Theses." Translated by C. M. Jacobs. In *Luther's Works*, edited by Helmut T. Lehmann, 25–33. Vol. 31. Philadelphia: Muhlenberg, 1957.

———. *Small Catechism*. Philadelphia: General Council Publication Board, 1874.

———. *The Table Talk of Martin Luther*. Edited by Thomas S. Kepler. Mineola, NY: Dover, 2005.

MacIntyre, Alasdair. *After Virtue: A Study in Moral Theory*. Notre Dame: University of Notre Dame Press, 1981.

McClendon, James Wm., Jr. "Baptism as a Performative Sign." *Theology Today* 23, no. 3 (October 1966): 403–416.

———. *Doctrine: Systematic Theology: Volume II*. Waco, TX: Baylor University Press, 2012.

Morris, Colin, and Peter Roberts, eds. *Pilgrimage: The English Experience from Becket to Bunyan*. Cambridge: Cambridge University Press, 2002.

Myers, Ben. *The Apostles' Creed: A Guide to the Ancient Catechism*. Bellingham, WA: Lexham Press, 2018.

Niebuhr, H. Richard. *The Kingdom of God in America*. New York: Harper, 1937. Reprint, Middletown, CT: Wesleyan University Press, 1988. Page references are to the 1988 edition.

Norris, Kathleen. *Amazing Grace*. New York: Riverhead Books, 1998.

Pelikan, Jaroslav. *Credo: Historical and Theological Guide to Creeds and Confessions of Faith in the Christian Tradition*. New Haven: Yale University Press, 2003.

Presbyterian Committee of Publication. *The Westminster Shorter Catechism*. Richmond, VA: Presbyterian Committee of Publication, 1862.

Rippon, John. *A Selection of Hymns from the Best Authors: Intended to Be an Appendix to Dr. Watts's Psalms and Hymns*. London: Thomas Wilkins, 1787.

Root, Kara K. "The 20-Second Gift of Washing Your Hands." *Faith & Leadership*, March 12, 2020. https://tinyurl.com/yddjrewa.

Sattler, Michael. *Schleitheim Articles*. Translated and edited by John H. Yoder. Scottdale, PA: Herald, 1973.

Smith, Christian, with Melinda Lundquist Denton. *Soul Searching: The Religious and Spiritual Lives of American Teenagers*. New York: Oxford University Press, 2005.

Smith, James K. A. *How (Not) to Be Secular: Reading Charles Taylor*. Grand Rapids: Eerdmans, 2014.

Spufford, Francis. *Unapologetic: Why, Despite Everything, Christianity Can Still Make Surprising Emotional Sense*. New York: Harper, 2013.

Taylor, Charles. *A Secular Age*. Cambridge: Belknap Press, 2007.

Tertullian. "Apology." Translated by S. Thelwall. In *The Ante-Nicene Fathers*, edited by A. Cleveland Coxe, 17–60. Vol. 3. Grand Rapids: Eerdmans, 1978.

———. "On Baptism." Translated by S. Thelwall. In *The Ante-Nicene Fathers*, edited by A. Cleveland Coxe, 669–679. Vol. 3. Grand Rapids: Eerdmans, 1978.

———. "On the Resurrection of the Flesh." Translated by Peter Holmes. In *The Ante-Nicene Fathers*, edited by A. Cleveland Coxe, 545–595. Vol. 3. Grand Rapids: Eerdmans, 1978.

Twain, Mark. *The Adventures of Huckleberry Finn*. New York: Puffin Books, 1994.

United Methodist Church. *The Book of Discipline of the United Methodist Church*. Nashville: United Methodist Publishing House, 2016.

W., Bill. *Alcoholics Anonymous*. 3rd ed. New York: Alcoholic Anonymous World Services, 1976.

Ward, Benedicta, trans. *The Sayings of the Desert Fathers*. Kalamazoo, MI: Cistercian, 1984.

Watts, Isaac. *Hymns and Spiritual Songs: In Three Books*. London: J. Humfreys for John Lawrence, 1709.

Wesley, John. "A Plain Account of Christian Perfection." In *Doctrinal and Controversial Treatises II*, edited by Paul Wesley Chilcote and Kenneth J. Collins. Vol. 13 of *The Works of John Wesley*. Nashville: Abingdon, 2013.

Wilkinson, John, ed. and trans. *Egeria's Travels to the Holy Land*. Rev. ed. Jerusalem: Ariel, 1981.

Williams, Rowan. *Resurrection*. New York: Pilgrim Press, 1984.

Wink, Walter. *Engaging the Powers: Discernment and Resistance in a World of Domination*. Minneapolis: Fortress Press, 1992.

Winslow, Edward. *Hypocrisie Unmasked*. London: Rich. Cotes, 1646. Reprint, New York: Burt Franklin, 1968. Page references are to the 1968 edition.

Wright, David P. "The Gesture of Hand Placement in the Hebrew Bible and in Hittite Literature." *Journal of the American Oriental Society* 106, no. 3 (July–September 1986): 433–446.

Topical Index

Scripture Index